Enquiry Skills

for GCSE

Karl Donert

HEINEMANN
EDUCATIONAL

Heinemann Educational,
a division of Heinemann Educational Books Ltd,
Halley Court, Jordan Hill, Oxford OX2 8EJ

OXFORD LONDON EDINBURGH
MELBOURNE SYDNEY AUCKLAND
IBADAN NAIROBI GABORONE HARARE
KINGSTON PORTSMOUTH N H (USA)
SINGAPORE MADRID BOLOGNA ATHENS

First published 1990

British Library Cataloguing in Publication Data

Donert, Karl
Enquiry skills for GCSE.
1. Geography. Field studies. Methodology.
I. Title
910'.724

ISBN 0 435 34011 5

Designed and produced by VAP Publishing Services,
Kidlington, Oxon

Printed and bound in Spain by Mateu Cromo

Acknowledgements

Grateful thanks are due to my wife, Nicole, for her support
and inspiration and for proof reading the final text and to
Fred Martin for his help and advice during the preparation
of this book.

The publishers would like to thank the following for
permission to reproduce copyright material: The Controller
of Her Majesty's Stationery Office © Crown Copyright for
the map extract from Landranger 115 (1:50000) on p. 21;
the map extract from Pathfinder SO 83/93 (1:25000) on p.
28; the map extract from Landranger OS Sheet 173
(1:50000) on p. 30; the map extract from Pathfinder 1198
ST 45/55 (1:25000) on p. 47; *Daily Telegraph* for the article
on p. 90; Midland Examining Group for the table on p. 4;
Oxford University Press for the flow map on p. 61.

The publishers would also like to thank the following for
permission to reproduce photographs: Heather Angel pp. 8,
21, 28, 53; Associated Press p. 90; J. Allan Cash pp. 7, 9
(bottom), 20 (top), 26, 31; Michael Jay Publications pp. 10
(right), 11 (thermometer); Fred Martin p. 18; Milton Keynes
Development Corporation p. 68; Oxford Scientific p. 41;
Topham Picture Library pp. 15, 20 (bottom), 34, 50; John
Walmsley pp. 4, 9 (top), 10 (left), 11, 14 (left), 16, 23, 35,
43, 71, 81, 86; Zefa/G. Mabbs p. 24; Zefa p. 32.

Cover photograph by John Walmsley.

Contents

Introduction: what is coursework?

COURSEWORK IS:

- a compulsory part of all geography courses
- worth at least 20% of the marks
- work produced during your GCSE course (Figure 1.1)
- marked/assessed by your teachers with a fixed mark scheme (Figure 1.2)
- checked in school to standardize the marks
- re-marked by an outside moderator.

Figure 1.1 *Coursework is work produced during your GCSE course*

COURSEWORK MUST:

- be your own work
- be relevant to the syllabus
- follow the guidelines of the syllabus
- be completed by the deadline set.

COURSEWORK CAN INCLUDE:

- a decision-making exercise
- a timed essay
- a structured exercise
- a fieldwork enquiry, which can be
  - an individual study
  - a teacher-led enquiry.

In some syllabuses, several pieces of coursework are required.

These statements of levels have been included in the syllabus to provide general guidance to teachers in both the setting and assessment of course work tasks. They are not intended to be definitive, but rather as draft guidelines which may require amendment in the light of experience.

LEVELS OF RESPONSE

	In a Geographical Enquiry of a simple nature.	In a Geographical Enquiry of Intermediate complexity.	In a Geographical Enquiry of complex nature.
Criterion (a) Primary and Secondary Data	**1–4 marks** The candidate has collected and recorded primary data on provided recording material by following precise instructions. The candidate has, where appropriate, selected relevant information from a limited number of secondary sources, given headings for guidance.	**1–8 marks** With guidance, the candidate has made geographically appropriate decisions about strategies for collecting and recording data, and has sucessfully carried them out. Including, where appropriate, selecting relevant information from a number of secondary sources.	**1–12 marks** The candidate has shown initiative in deciding what data is required and how to record it appropriately in relation to the objectives of the Enquiry. The candidate has received only general guidance and occasional tutoring when sought.
Criterion (b) Presentation of Data	**1–4 marks** The candidate has presented and refined the data in a limited but appropriate form as a result of step by step instructions.	**1–8 marks** With guidance, the candidate has chosen and used a number of geographically appropriate techniques to process and present the data.	**1–12 marks** Given limited guidance, the candidate has presented and refined the collected data chosen or devised appropriate graphical, cartographical and/or numerical forms.
Criterion (c) Analysis, Interpretation	**1–5 marks** With specific guidance, the candidate has attempted limited analysis of the refined data and shown some simple awareness of the relevance of the values and perceptions of decision makers.	**1–10 marks** Given guidance, the candidate has analysed the refined data and used geographical concepts and principles to offer some interpretation, including demonstrating an understanding of the importance of values and perceptions in decision making.	**1–14 marks** The candidate has demonstrated the ability to analyse and interpret data by applying geographical concepts and principles. The candidate has demonstrated an understanding of the role of decision making and the values and perceptions of decision makers in the evolution of patterns in human geography.
Criterion (d) Conclusions	**1–4 marks** The candidate has presented a commentary expressed basically in descriptive terms, with very limited comment on the application and usefulness of the findings.	**1–8 marks** The candidate has drawn some conclusions and presented, where appropriate, proposals, justification and evaluations for solutions to geographical problems.	**1–12 marks** The candidate has drawn conclusions and discussed possible implications. The candidate has shown initiative and imagination in drawing up and evaluating proposals for solutions to geographical problems where appropriate.

Figure 1.2 *A coursework mark scheme*

Things to do

Make a copy of Figure 1.3 and fill in the details about your GCSE geography course and the coursework it involves.

Figure 1.3 *Your GCSE Geography course*

Syllabus title		Exam group	
Syllabus code		Percentage coursework	
How many pieces of coursework must I do?			
What is each piece of coursework about?		**What is each piece worth?**	
1		1	
2		2	
3		3	
4		4	
5		5	
6		6	
When must I finish my coursework?			

COURSEWORK MEANS THAT:

work throughout the course counts towards your final grade
fieldwork involving the collection of data is a compulsory part of all GCSE geography courses

- a proportion of your marks will be decided before the end of the course
- a variety of activities are included in the course.

Things to do

Grade yourself between 0 and 5 on each of these questions.

bad   good
0   1   2   3   4   5

1 How good are you at working on your own?
2 How do you feel about working as part of a group?
3 How good are you at following instructions?
4 How well do you organize your ideas?
5 How good are you at collecting information?
6 How well do you communicate with others in your class?
7 What do you think of drawing maps, sketches and graphs?
8 How do you feel about producing a piece of original work?
9 How well do you present your work?
10 How good are you at handing in work on time?

These skills are all required in geography coursework and you will need to master them.

2 *Choosing a suitable topic*

Figure 2.1
Some geographical themes

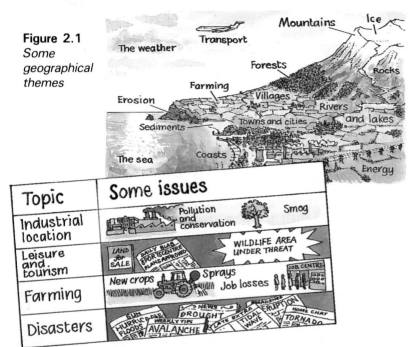

Figure 2.2 *Some geographical topics and issues*

THEMES

Geography covers a vast range of study themes (Figure 2.1). These themes are all suitable starting points for a geographical enquiry.

There are three types of theme:
● **physical** (or **environmental**) themes
● **human** themes
● **issues**, the inter-relationships between human and physical themes.

Figure 2.2 shows some geographical issues. They can all be good topics for study. Make a list of other geographical themes which you could study.

Figure 2.3 *Scales of study*

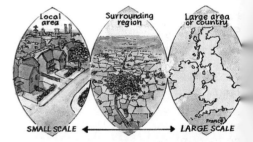

SCALE OF STUDY

The scale of your study is linked with the size of your study area (Figure 2.3).

Fieldwork enquiries must be your own work and you must collect your own data. Since this can only be done locally, it is best to aim at studying your local area. You should then look at the wider implications of your study.

Always look at a specific issue or problem.

The time scale of your enquiry is also important. You will have to complete your enquiry before the end of your GCSE course.

ASKING QUESTIONS

Once you have chosen your topic, you need to ask questions in order to give yourself ideas. Local features or events may have interested you – now is the time to find out about them. If you decide to look at a specific problem, it needs to be broken down into manageable pieces for you to study.

Things to do

1 Make a list of the physical and human themes that are involved in these issues:
   a flooding
   b rubbish disposal
   c earthquakes.

2 a Which of the subjects below would not make a suitable topic for a fieldwork enquiry?
      (i) a river meander
      (ii) British Rail
      (iii) a supermarket
      (iv) a factory
      (v) a farm
      (vi) national weather
   b Explain why.
   c How would you alter these unsuitable subjects so that you could study them?

HYPOTHESIS

Once you have decided on the question you want to answer, you should predict what you would expect to happen under normal conditions. This prediction is called a **hypothesis** (Figure 2.4).

Your hypothesis should be written out and, sometimes, can also be represented by a graph.

Geographical enquiries are therefore based around an **idea** that can be studied. Here are some examples:

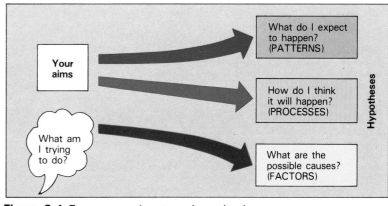

Figure 2.4 *From your aims to a hypothesis*

Subject: Public and private transport.

Question: When are park-and-ride facilities used in a small town?

Hypothesis: The use of park-and-ride increases during the day until 3 p.m. when it declines.

Subject: Weather.

Question: Where in a valley does fog occur?

Hypothesis: Fog most commonly occurs close to rivers.

SUBJECT	BEACH PEBBLES
QUESTIONS	
HYPOTHESES	
SUBJECT	TRAFFIC LIGHTS
QUESTIONS	
HYPOTHESES	

AIMS

Present a list of things you:
- are trying to do
- want to find out
- need to survey
- your study.

It is vital that your list of aims is checked by your teacher. Try not to set yourself too much to do – don't be too ambitious.

3 Copy Figure 2.5.

4 a Fill in the table for the two photographs (Figures 2.6 and 2.7).
  b What questions might you ask?
  c What hypothesis might you have?
  d What do you think is happening at each location?

For your own enquiry:

5 Decide which geographical themes interest you and which questions you would want to study in your enquiry.

6 List carefully the aims of your own enquiry. What are you trying to do?

7 Make an extra copy of Figure 2.5 and fill it in for your own enquiry.

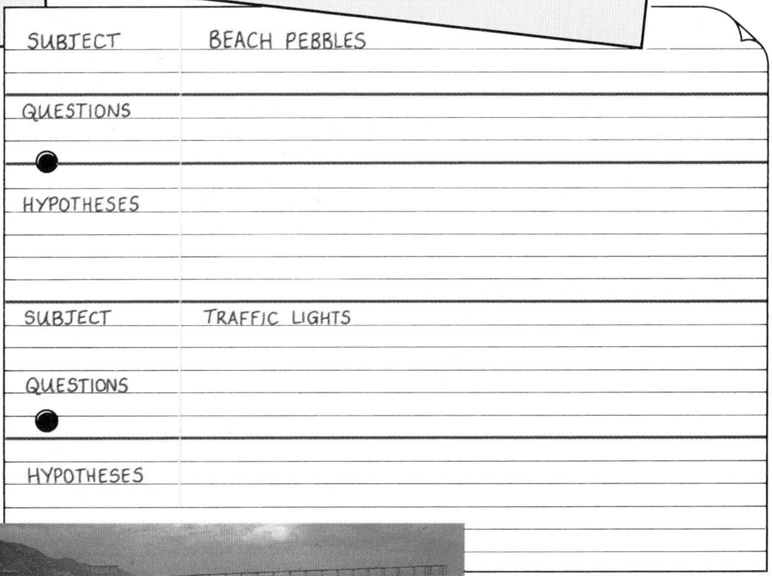

Figure 2.5 *A page from a notebook*

Figure 2.6

Figure 2.7

Experimental design

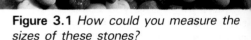

Figure 3.1 *How could you measure the sizes of these stones?*

WHAT SHOULD I SURVEY?

USING MEASUREMENTS

There are several ways of measuring things. To choose the right method, you need to know exactly what you are looking for, so it is very important that you make the right decision.

How you decide to measure will affect the amount and type of equipment you may need. It will alter the amount of time it will take you to survey. It also influences the accuracy of your results.

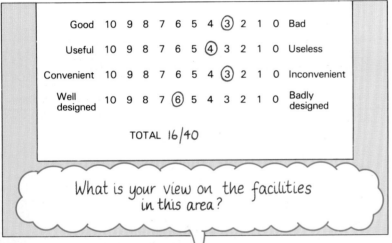

Figure 3.2 *Designing an index*

PHYSICAL MEASUREMENTS

Example: stone size (Figure 3.1) can be measured in a number of ways:
- weight
- diameter
- volume.

What equipment would you need to measure stone size in these three ways? Which would be the quickest for you to measure in the field?

In some cases special equipment will be necessary. Make a list of examples of special equipment which you have seen or used.

PEOPLE'S OPINIONS AND VALUES

The views we have are often the basis for study. The way we interpret our surroundings is called our **perception**. This depends on many things, including our age, upbringing and even the weather!

It is very difficult to obtain accurate and unbiased results unless the questions asked during the survey are well designed. This type of enquiry can lead to very interesting surveys, but they are difficult to do well. Designing an index to measure views and values may give the best results.

CONSTRUCTING AN INDEX

An index is a number which is used to measure how people feel about what is being surveyed, for example how satisfied people are with facilities in their local area (Figure 3.2).

To draw up an index:

1 list the things which you think are relevant
2 ask yourself how important each of the factors are
3 construct your index by combining these factors.

Things to do

1 Make a list of the ways that you could measure building size.

2 Design an index which would give you a measure of how accessible different areas are to the centre of a town.

3 a List the factors that you would take into account to study the appearance and condition of the buildings where you live.
  b Draw up an index that you could use to measure it.

QUANTITIES

In most cases a survey that gives numbers for its results will be the easiest to present and to deal with later. Numbers can be easily compared. When designing your enquiry make sure you consider all the possible ways of obtaining your results before making your final decision (Figure 3.3).

Things to do

1 Make a list of the geographical skills being practised in Figure 3.5.

2 You have to survey the river in Figure 3.5 and measure the water speed. (Speed is the distance the water travels over a certain time.)
   a What skills would be necessary to obtain this information?
   b How might you measure river speed?
   c What equipment would you need?
   d In what units would you measure river speed?
   e If the river channel was very shallow, what difficulties might there be in measuring river speed?
   f What other measurements would you make about the river and its valley in order to understand why river speed varies?

3 You are asked to survey the shops in the High Street shown in Figure 3.6 to find out people's views about them and which ones they use most.
   a What skills are needed for this exercise?
   b What possible ways are there for you to obtain this information?
   c Suggest what problems might result.
   d If you were working as part of a group to collect this information, what other skills would you need?

For your own enquiry:
4 Copy the checklist (Figure 3.7). Answer the questions to help you design your enquiry.

Figure 3.7 Checklist: designing an enquiry

SKILLS

GCSE concentrates on **skills**. Skills are abilities that you will acquire and improve by practice. What skills would you normally link with geography?

A list of some geographical skills are given in Figure 3.4.

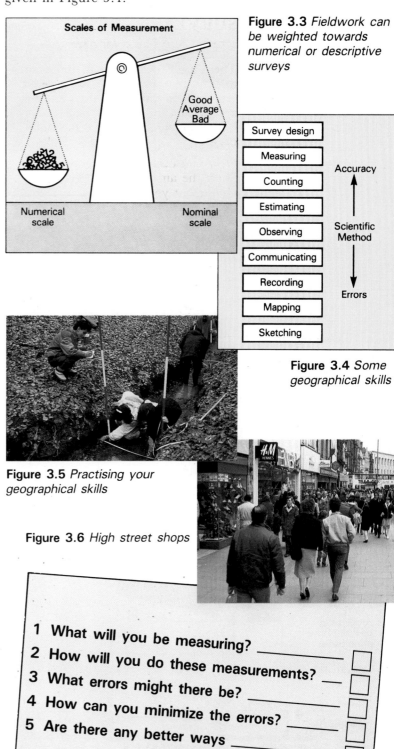

Figure 3.3 Fieldwork can be weighted towards numerical or descriptive surveys

Figure 3.4 Some geographical skills

Figure 3.5 Practising your geographical skills

Figure 3.6 High street shops

1 What will you be measuring? _____
2 How will you do these measurements? __
3 What errors might there be? _____
4 How can you minimize the errors? _____
5 Are there any better ways _____

4 Equipment

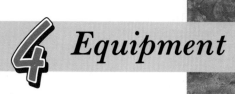

Figure 4.1 *A flowmeter*

Figure 4.2 *A meter for measuring light intensity*

TYPES OF EQUIPMENT

You will need equipment for most fieldwork enquiries. Many different types of equipment are available. Most of the equipment is used in physical and environmental surveys.

Some simple items are needed for most surveys. These include pencils and Biros, rulers, and drawing equipment such as a protractor.

Remember that clothing is an important part of the equipment you will need. Be sensible about your choice of clothing. It is better to have too much clothing to wear than too little. If in doubt, ask your teacher for advice about the conditions you are likely to be surveying in and what clothing you will need.

Two examples of equipment which are commonly used in fieldwork are shown in Figures 4.1 and 4.2. This equipment allows you to make direct measurements, so no calculations are involved.

In most cases, however, you will need to make calculations from your measurements. For example, in Figures 4.3 and 4.4, the width, height and slope are obtained by making calculations from other measurements.

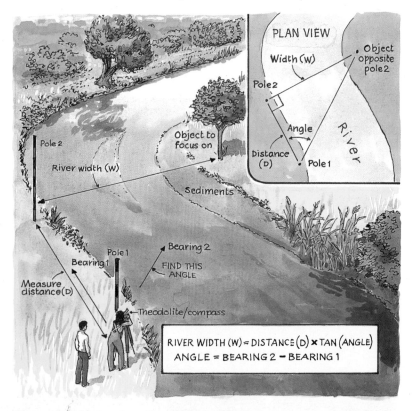

Figure 4.3 *Measuring river width indirectly*

RIVER WIDTH (W) = DISTANCE (D) ✕ TAN (ANGLE)
ANGLE = BEARING 2 − BEARING 1

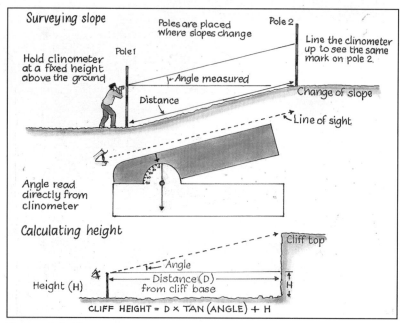

Figure 4.4 *Measuring slope and calculating height*

CLIFF HEIGHT = D ✕ TAN (ANGLE) + H

Things to do

1 Classify the equipment shown in Figures 4.1 and 4.2 under the headings cost, size, how easy they are to use, their necessity, speed of use and how simple they are.

2 Compare the equipment shown in Figures 4.5 and 4.6 with those in Figures 4.1 and 4.2.

DO IT YOURSELF

It may often be possible to make your own survey equipment. For example, selecting samples is normally done by using a **quadrat**. This is used to locate survey sites on maps or placed on the ground to obtain samples (Figure 4.5). Range poles, large rulers, Stevenson's screens and rain gauges are also simple to make from commonly found objects (Figure 4.6). You can also make more complex equipment (Figure 4.7).

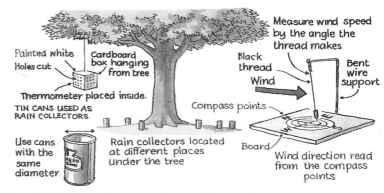

Figure 4.6 *Some home-made weather equipment*

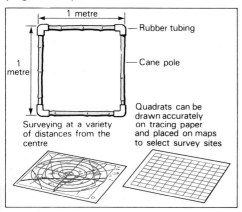

Figure 4.5 *DIY quadrats*

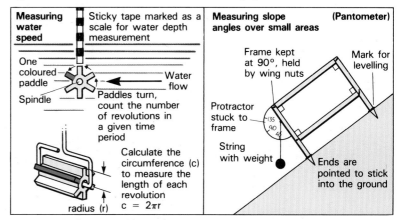

Figure 4.7 *Some more complicated DIY equipment*

Things to do

1 **a** Make a copy of the table below.
   b Study Figure 4.8 and complete your table by spotting the equipment and filling in what it is used for.

'Spot the equipment'		
number	name	use
1		
2		
3		
4		
5		
6		

2 Design and draw a labelled diagram of a piece of equipment that you could make and use to:
   a catch sediments at the bottom of a small stream
   b measure the amount of water running down the trunk of a tree during a storm.

Figure 4.8 *Spot the equipment*

5 Using equipment

Figure 5.1
Using equipment

The sportsman

The scientist

The businessman

Only one previous owner

The mountaineer

The adventurer

The intellectual

$E=MC^2$

The geographer

Before collecting data using equipment, you need to:
- check that the equipment works
- know how to take care of it (is it fragile?)
- understand how to use it
- know what it measures
- know what units it is measuring in (if any).

SKILLS

The **skills** involved when using equipment can include:
- designing and testing equipment
- reading a scale
- recording information
- measuring
- estimating accuracy
- computing and calculating
- using personal initiative.

Look at Figure 5.1. Where do you fit in?

WEATHER INSTRUMENTS

Many schools have their own weather station (Figure 5.2) and this may be a valuable source of information for a fieldwork enquiry. They are set up to measure the weather at one point.

Weather instruments should avoid trees, walls, and direct heat and sunlight unless you are specifically interested in studying them. If you are trying to compare a number of places, then you need to make sure that the equipment you use is the same size and in a similar position at each place.

The pressure, temperature, humidity, precipitation, sunshine, cloud and wind might all form the basis of a good enquiry. Records may have been kept from the weather station and these might be a very useful secondary source of data.

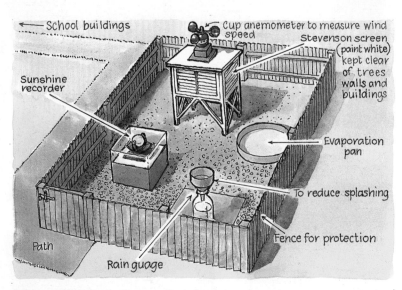

School buildings

Cup anemometer to measure wind speed

Stevenson screen (paint white) kept clear of trees walls and buildings

Sunshine recorder

Evaporation pan

To reduce splashing

Fence for protection

Path

Rain guage

Figure 5.2 *Layout for a school weather station*

LABORATORY WORK

Samples collected in the field may
need to be investigated in the
laboratory.

SAFETY IN THE LABORATORY
- Working with chemicals can be
  dangerous.
- Be careful with electrical
  equipment.
- You may need to use an oven –
  don't burn yourself!

GOOD PRACTICE
- Get permission to use the
  laboratory.
- Keep equipment clean.
- Repeat your survey if necessary.
- If weighing, zero the balance.
- Be organized, know what you are
  doing and why.
- Remember the units.
- Tidy up afterwards.

EXAMPLES
1 sieving sediments (Figure 5.3)
2 soil analysis (Figure 5.4)

Things to do

1 What local conditions might affect
the results given by the weather
equipment in Figure 5.2?

2 What are the units for:
a air temperature
b rainfall
c wave height
d gradient (or slope)?

For your own enquiry:
3 Make a copy of the equipment
checklist (Figure 5.5) for your field
notebook.

4 Make a list of equipment you will
need to take with you for your
survey.

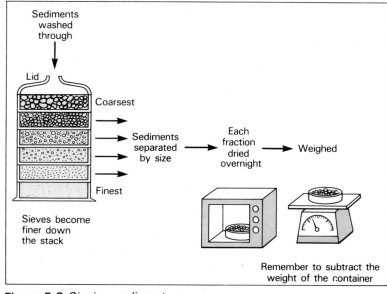

Figure 5.3 *Sieving sediments*

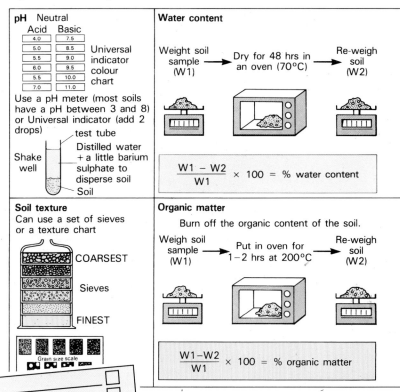

Figure 5.4 *Soil analysis*

1 Does it work? _____
2 What does it measure? _____
3 What units does it measure in? _____
4 Is it relevant to my study? _____
5 Is it feasible? _____
6 Can I use it? _____
7 Are there alternatives? _____
8 What are they? _____
9 Are any of them better/easier? _____
10 Will I have enough time? _____
11 Is it breakable? _____
12 What happens if . . . ? _____
13 Don't lose it! _____
14 Don't leave it behind! _____

List

?

Figure 5.5 *Equipment checklist*

Recording information

THE FIELD NOTEBOOK

For any enquiry, you need to keep a full and detailed account of the survey, its location and any events. This is a record of all the information which may be useful when your enquiry is written up. This record is called a field notebook (Figure 6.1).

Figure 6.1 *The field notebook*

Your field notebook should include:
● any sketches or profiles of the survey area
● the survey sheets on which you collected the data
● a full list of any observations you made while carrying out the survey
● details of any specimens
● a note of any special events
● the names of any contacts
● a list of any ideas or views you have
● a list of photographs you have taken.

Make sure you leave lots of empty spaces in your notebook in case you need to write or draw things in later.

PREPARATION

Before any survey a number of things need to be prepared. Preparing your field notebook before your survey can save you a lot of time in the field. Figure 6.2 is a checklist of some of the preparations which may be necessary. Write out a copy of this checklist and keep it inside your field notebook.

Figure 6.2 *Checklist: preparation*

1 **What equipment will I need?** _____ ☐	
2 **Do I know how to use the equipment?** _____ ☐	
3 **What survey sheets/ questionnaires should I use?** _____ ☐	
4 **How many surveys should I use?** _____ ☐	
5 **Prepare sheets/ questionnaires.** _____ ☐	
6 **Check equipment is working.** _____ ☐	

PROTECT YOUR DATA
● Use a pencil or Biro rather than a fountain pen.
● Carry spare pens, paper and survey sheets.
● Use a plastic sheet over your notebook to keep out the rain (Figure 6.3).

Figure 6.3 *Keep out the rain*

SURVEY SHEETS

Survey results are filled in on sheets which you have prepared before doing your fieldwork (Figure 6.4). All the information you collect should be filled in along with a careful note of where the survey was carried out. Leave enough space to fill in all the results. A well designed survey sheet can save you a lot of time. It also makes mistakes less likely.

Survey sheets must have:
● headings, including the units you measured in
● survey data
● space for comments.

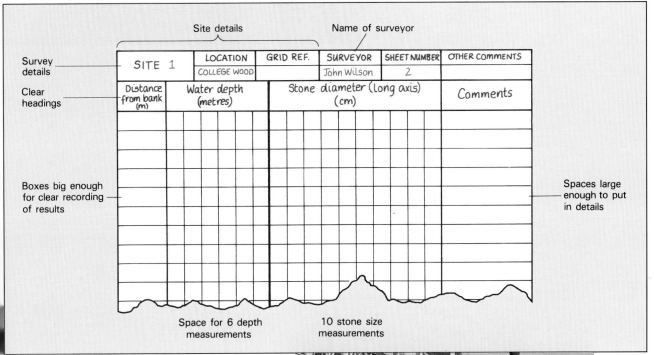

Figure 6.4 *The survey sheet*

Things to do

1 What helps make the headings in Figure 6.4 clear and easy to read?

2 If you are working with others in a group, how could you avoid confusion over who handed in any survey sheets you can't read or understand?

3 Redraw the headings in Figure 6.4 to include a sketch of the area being surveyed. Leave enough space for the drawing to be labelled.

4 You are surveying how people use a small pedestrian shopping precinct (Figure 6.5). You have decided to count the number of people who use each of the shops shown between 2 p.m. and 5 p.m. Your aim is to see how the number of shoppers varies during the afternoon.

Figure 6.5

a Draw up a survey sheet which you could use to record the number of shoppers going into each shop every 15 minutes.

b What other details might you notice and write down during the afternoon which could explain your results?

For your own enquiry:

5 Make a list of important things to prepare for your survey.

6 What observations must you make about your survey area?

7 Prepare your survey sheets and field notebook.

7 Questionnaires

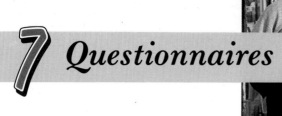

Figure 7.1 *Carrying out a street survey*

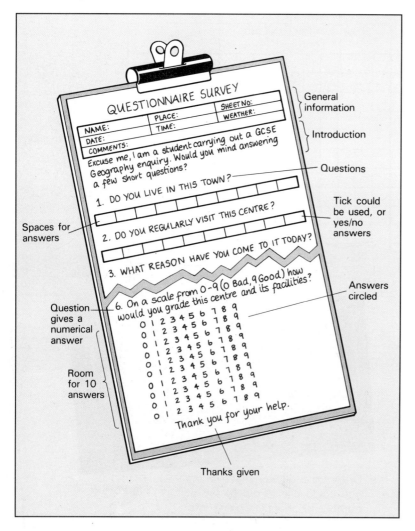

Figure 7.2 *Designing your questionnaire*

Questionnaire surveys are used for obtaining opinions, views, ideas and information about the way people behave. They are used by market researchers, salespersons, politicians and canvassers.

There are four ways that questionnaires can be done:
1 on the street
2 door-to-door
3 by post
4 by telephone.

You will probably only use street questionnaires during your coursework (Figure 7.1).

HOW TO DESIGN YOUR SURVEY

- Include an introduction on the questionnaire sheet. This should say who you are and what you are doing (Figure 7.2).
- Leave spaces for answers on the sheet. It is better to have too much space than not enough.
- Prepare your sheets so that you only have to underline or circle answers. This will save time.
- Try to write the questions so that they give simple yes/no answers or lead to a precise statement. This will avoid vague, unclear results.
- Avoid interview bias – make sure you obtain *their* views, not yours.

Questionnaires test your **organization** and **communication** skills.

Questionnaires involve both questions and answers.

a few
short
uncomplicated
sensible
} **QUESTIONS**

WHICH GIVE:

clear
precise
quantitative
   (or numerical)
} **ANSWERS**

Things to do

1 **a** From Figure 7.1, where is the survey being done?
   b Do there appear to be any problems with the survey?

2 When do you think people are most likely to refuse to answer your questions?

Things to do

1 **a** Write an introduction to a questionnaire. Include your school, the purpose of your interview and roughly how long the interview will take.
  b Try out your introduction on other members of your class. Did they have any suggestions for how to improve it?

2 Now compare the good and bad interview questions (Figure 7.3) which were prepared by pupils for a shopping survey outside a large hypermarket. Suggest why the questions are labelled good and bad.

3 Look at the survey questions (Figure 7.4) for a shopping enquiry. Try to alter the questions so that they result in precise, numerical answers. Answers which are *not* based on people's views are required, unless their opinions are actually asked for.

4 **a** Design a questionnaire which finds out the ways people use a local park or playground near where you live, and their views on what facilities need to be added. Use the checklist in Figure 7.5.
  b In pairs, test your questionnaire in class.
  c Comment on the answers you obtain. Were they what you expected?

  You may need to improve your questionnaire by rewording it or altering the questions you ask.

Figure 7.3 *Good and bad questions*

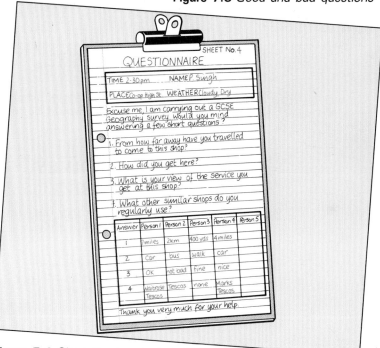

Figure 7.4 *Shopping survey questions*

1 Identify what information you need. _____ ☐
2 How should the questions be worded? _____ ☐
3 Write trial questionnaire. _____ ☐
4 Carry out small trial survey. _____ ☐
5 Alter/improve questions. _____ ☐
6 Write up/copy final version. _____ ☐

Figure 7.5 *Checklist: questionnaires*

Survey types (taking a sample)

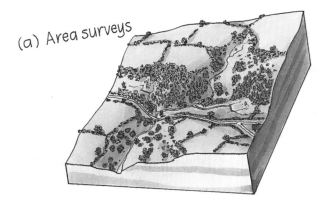

(a) Area surveys

Surveys done in different parts of the valley

Figure 8.1 *The two main types of survey*

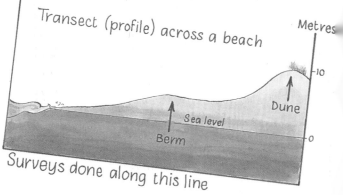

(b) Line surveys

Transect (profile) across a beach

Metres

Dune

Sea level

Berm

Surveys done along this line

Figure 8.1 shows the two main types of survey. In your enquiry you need to decide whether you are investigating a whole area or whether a line across that area would be more suitable.

WHERE TO SURVEY, AND SURVEY SIZE

The place where you carry out your survey has to be chosen carefully (Figure 8.2).

The size of your survey is also important. A complete or 100 per cent questionnaire survey of the people living in an area is usually

impossible because of the time involved. Similarly, a survey of all the stones on the small beach in Figure 8.3 would not be practical. Instead you need to design a method to select what you will survey and where. This is called **sampling**. The sample to survey is selected from within the whole area (or population).

Figure 8.3 *Why wouldn't a survey of all the stones on this beach be practical?*

Figure 8.2 *Checklist: survey site*

1 Is the site easy to get to?
2 Are there any dangers?
3 Do I have to get permission?
4 Is the site suitable for my survey?
5 Are there any special reasons for surveying at this site?

You need to choose the sample you are going to survey before doing your fieldwork. The survey locations must be **representative**. This means it needs to be typical of the whole area, line or population you are studying. Surveying shops on a Wednesday afternoon after 4 p.m. is unlikely to give you the shopping pattern for the whole week. Measuring stones by a river bank is unlikely to give you a realistic picture of the sediments in the whole channel.

Understanding the needs of the enquiry will play a big part in choosing where you will survey. The location and type of sample must fit the requirements of your study and the time you have to collect your results.

How big your survey should be is not an easy decision to make. If there are too many surveys, it will take too much time to finish. If there are too few then the results will not be very valuable. Finding the right balance is important (Figure 8.4).

TYPES OF SAMPLE

Figure 8.5 shows the four types of sampling which you can use.

Figure 8.4 *Finding the balance*

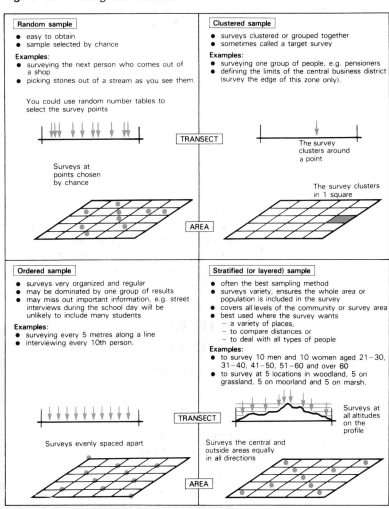

Figure 8.5 *The four types of sampling*

Things to do

1 Which type of sample surveys:
   a in one place
   b a complete cross-section
   c by chance
   d in the most logical way?

2 Which type of survey would you carry out if you wanted to find out how pupils travel to and from your school? Explain the reasons for your choice.

3 You have decided to study the stone size around the base of a scree.
   a Would you use an area or transect survey?
   b Which sample type would you use?
   c How many stones would you survey at each site?
   d How many sites would you survey?

4 Check your answers to question 3 with others in your class.
   a How do your answers compare?
   b Is your survey too big or too small?
   c Have you chosen the right balance?
   d Is your survey a representative one?

9 *Before you start*

Figure 9.1 *A busy main road*

Figure 9.2 *A fast flowing river*

Units 9 – 19 deal with the practicalities and problems that arise during fieldwork and the collection of data. Units 11 to 18 give detailed examples of surveys in a variety of geographical themes and issues.

BE SAFE: TAKE NO RISKS

When you do fieldwork you will need to collect information in all sorts of places. Always make sure you are not in any danger.

Look at Figures 9.1 and 9.2 carefully. Write out a list of possible dangers at each site. Can you think of any other possible dangerous places?

PREPARATION

Before you do fieldwork it is a good idea to do as much preparation as possible. Things you can do in advance include:

- looking at maps of your chosen area
- writing survey sheets
- preparing your field notebook
- visiting your survey area if you can
- doing a trial survey, making sketches, taking photographs
- getting permission to do the fieldwork
- checking you have sensible clothing and footwear
- checking you have all the equipment you need.

You should also tell someone where you are going and when you will be there. Make sure you carry identification at all times (Figure 9.3). Identification should include who you are, your address, telephone number and school.

ID CARD
Name   J. MERCER
School   ST. JOHNS
School address   PARK ROAD, LUXTON
Phone No.   916340
Home address   49, LEE CRESCENT, LUXTON

Photograph

School stamp

ST JOHNS SCHOOL   Date 12.9.89

Figure 9.3 *Always carry your ID*

CHOOSING SURVEY SITES

You need to choose the sites for your survey very carefully because they could seriously affect your results. Try to pick sites which give an idea of the area as a whole. This is called a **representative survey**.

Figure 9.4

Things to do

Study Figures 9.4 to 9.7.

1 Which part of Figure 9.4 is not representative of the area as a whole?

2 Figure 9.5 is a sketch of a coastal sand dune transect. You plan to do a survey of the sediments and vegetation. Which parts would you need to survey to give a representative survey?

3 The sketch map (Figure 9.6) shows an area to be surveyed. In choosing survey sites in this area, what might be important other than the tree? List the effects they could have.

4 You want to carry out a river survey in the area shown in Figure 9.7.
   a Give the grid references of any areas you think might be dangerous for carrying out surveys.
   b Where are the best access points?
   c Where can you cross the river?
   d Are there any places on the river which you would not survey? Say where they are and explain your reasons.

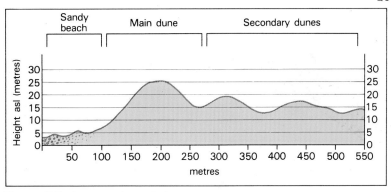

Figure 9.5 *A coastal sand dune transect*

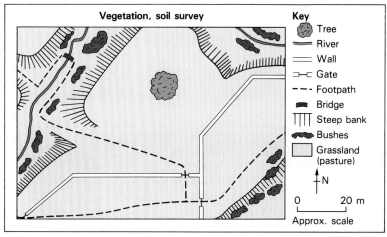

Figure 9.6 *Sketch map for a vegetation and soil survey*

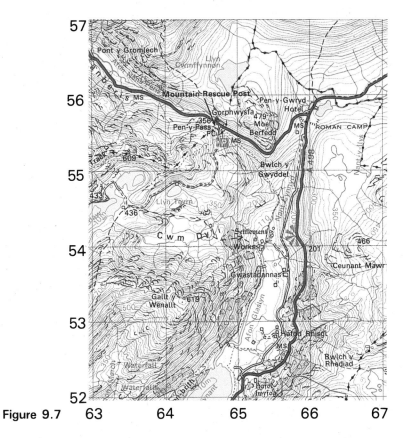

Figure 9.7

10 Measurement and accuracy

OBSERVATION

It is important, when collecting data, to observe what is happening very carefully (Figure 10.1). This can be done as a measurement or just a comment which describes what you see. This comment could be very important in explaining your results. Make sure you leave plenty of space for this on your survey sheets (Figure 10.2) or in your field notebook.

Figure 10.1 *Measure accurately!*

TAKING MEASUREMENTS

Surveyed information can be either descriptive or numerical (Figure 10.3).

Figure 10.3 *Surveyed information can either descriptive or numerical*

COLLECTING DATA

Here are some useful rules for collecting data:

- number your survey sheets so that you can keep them in order
- write down your results clearly
- leave plenty of space for additional comments

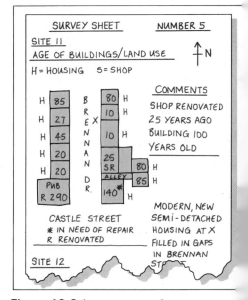

Figure 10.2 *Leave space for comments*

If you are taking numerical measurements:
- make sure you know how to use the equipment you will need (practise using the equipment and carry out a trial survey)
- remember to write down the unit you have measured in
- measure everything several times, to reduce errors
- note down where each measurement was taken from.

Be as accurate as you can – your survey is only as good as the *least* accurate measurements you make.

Errors	Random errors	Systematic errors
Why they happen?	Happen by chance – your survey may collect data which doesn't show the real situation.	Errors which happen frequently because you are doing something wrong or using equipment which isn't working properly.
How to avoid or reduce them	Can be reduced by increasing the number of times you do your survey.	Check your methods and equipment thoroughly before you begin.

Figure 10.4 *Two types of error*

AVOIDING ERRORS

Figure 10.4 shows two types of error which can occur when collecting data.

Figure 10.5 *A rain gauge and measuring cylinder*

Things to do

1 Look at Figure 10.5
   a What is the reading on the rain gauge?
   b How accurately can you read it?
   c Why should you place rain gauges away from trees and buildings?

2 List six things in Figure 10.6 which show poor survey skills. Give reasons for your choice.

3 Study Power's stone roundness classification table (Figure 10.7).
   a Classify the six stones in Figure 10.7 using Power's roundness scale.
   b Compare your results with those of the rest of the class.
   c Is this a numerical or descriptive classification? How useful is it? What problems does it have?

4 a Devise an index for assessing the quality of housing in different residential areas in a town.
   b Is an index a numerical or a descriptive measure?

Figure 10.6 *How not to carry out a survey!*

Poor survey skills

I make it 12·069 metres

Oh hurry up! Let's get back

This river is only 1 step wide

I've no more space for results

I'll survey about here

These flowers are nice

My ink is running out I can't read my results

I forgot the last number. Oh never mind

54·75 inches OK

Figure 10.7 *Power's roundness scale*

A Very angular   C Sub-angular   E Rounded
B Angular   D Sub-rounded   F Well rounded

11 *A traffic survey*

Subject: Road transport

Questions: How does the amount and type of road traffic vary at one point during the day? (Figure 11.1).
Why do the differences occur?

Hypotheses: Traffic will be greatest during the rush hours in the morning and evening.
The proportion of lorries in the traffic will increase between these peak times.

Figure 11.1

WHAT TO MEASURE

The amount and type of traffic is the key to this enquiry. To get traffic flows you will need to count vehicles over a fixed time period, like 10 minutes.

You could split the type of traffic into:
A 2-wheeled – bicycles, mopeds, etc.
B 4-wheeled – cars, vans
C 4-wheeled – lorries
D Large vehicles – buses, large lorries, etc.
E Total vehicles = A + B + C + D
This is the amount of traffic.

SURVEY DETAILS

Survey away from crossroads, where vehicles leaving and joining the road can cause confusion. Position yourself where you can count the vehicles easily and clearly. Avoid bus stops and places where large lorries stop.

Survey traffic for 10 minutes, counting the number of each type of vehicle. Repeat the survey after a 5 minute interval. Do as many surveys as possible at different times of the day.

To help you keep count, prepare your field notebook so that you can write down your results as you go along. See Figure 11.2.

Figure 11.2 *Prepare your field notebook*

field Notebook.					Page 6
Date: 17/3/88		**Start Time :** 11·15			
A	B	C	D	Total (E)	Comments
11	LHT LHT LHT LHT	LHT 11	1		Policeman
					controlling
					traffic after
				43	accident.

Figure 11.3 *A road survey: survey sheet*

SURVEY SHEET 3						
Date: 17 March		**Location:** Silver St. Outside Chemists				
Weather: Sunny, dry		**Other Comments:** Not a market day, but busy.				
Time	A	B	C	D	Total E	Comments
10·00—10·10	1	37	3	0	41	
10·15—10·25	0	44	6	1	51	
10·30—10·40	2	41	5	0	49	Lorry slowed traffic
10·45—10·55	0	60	4	0	64	
11·00—11·10	3	46	6	1	55	
11·15—11·25	2	33	7	1	43	Accident at 11·25
11·30—11·40	1	1	0	0	2	
11·45—11·55	4	12	0	0	16	Road cleared 11·50
12·00—12·10						Traffic Jam.
12·15—12·25						

PREPARATION

Prepare your survey sheets (Figure 11.3).

Prepare your field notebook.

Choose your survey location.

Draw a sketch map of the survey location.

Watch/stopwatch.

Figure 11.4 *Some unexpected problems counting traffic*

POINTS TO REMEMBER
- Keep clear of dangerous road areas. Stand back.
- Avoid very large roads or traffic flows (Figure 11.4).
- Shelter may be useful, if it is wet.

Things to do

1 If you were carrying out this survey, how would you classify each of the forms of transport shown in Figure 11.5?

Study the sketch map of a town centre (Figure 11.6).

2 Write a hypothesis which suggests what effect
a the factory
b the school
might have on traffic flows between 8.30 a.m. and 4 p.m. on the main roads.

3 a Sketch a graph of the total traffic flow you would expect outside the theatre on King Street through the day (8 a.m. to 8 p.m.).
b On your graph, mark the highest and lowest traffic flows you expect.
c Write an explanation of the graph you have drawn.

4 If you wanted to study the uses of the car parks in Figure 11.6:
a What possible uses might each of them have?
b Design a survey to look at the uses of the different car parks in the area.
c Draw a survey sheet which you could use to collect data for one of these car parks.

Figure 11.6 *Sketch map of King St. and the main roads surrounding it*

Figure 11.5 *Some different vehicle types*

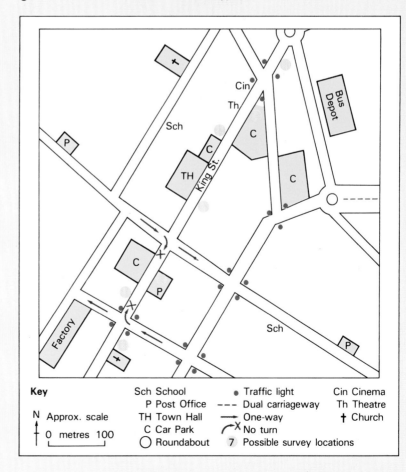

Key

Sch School	• Traffic light	Cin Cinema
P Post Office	--- Dual carriageway	Th Theatre
N Approx. scale	TH Town Hall	→ One-way	✝ Church
0 metres 100	C Car Park	✗ No turn	
	○ Roundabout	7 Possible survey locations	

12 *Pedestrians and shopping*

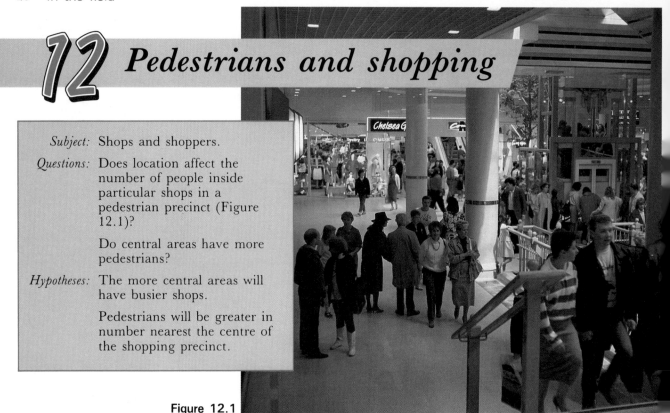

Subject: Shops and shoppers.

Questions: Does location affect the number of people inside particular shops in a pedestrian precinct (Figure 12.1)?

Do central areas have more pedestrians?

Hypotheses: The more central areas will have busier shops.

Pedestrians will be greater in number nearest the centre of the shopping precinct.

Figure 12.1

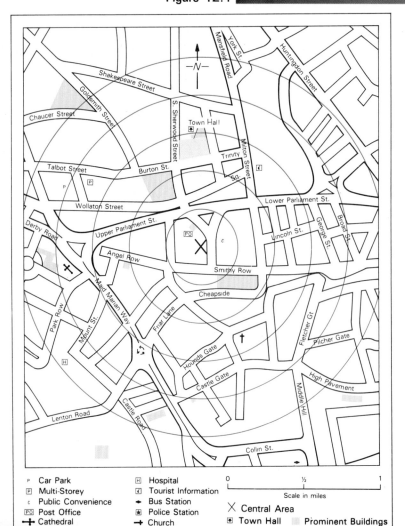

WHAT TO MEASURE

You must first decide where the centre of the shopping area is. This can be done by selecting an important building such as the town hall, or working out the central location from a map (Figure 12.2).

You need to survey a variety of different shops in the shopping precinct and to count the pedestrians passing each shop that is being surveyed. The number of shoppers inside the shop can be counted straight after the pedestrian count.

SURVEY DETAILS

Use a stratified sample of shops, selecting shops at different distances from the centre. You should survey each shop six times. Select as many shops as possible, but include at leas ten shops. Count the pedestrians for 5 minutes. Then count the number of shoppers inside the shop.

Position yourself where people passing the shop can be counted easily. If you need to go inside the shop, don't forget that permission will be needed (Figure 12.3).

p	Car Park	H	Hospital
P	Multi-Storey	i	Tourist Information
c	Public Convenience		Bus Station
PO	Post Office		Police Station
+	Cathedral		Church

✕ Central Area
⊞ Town Hall   Prominent Buildings

0   ½   1
Scale in miles

Figure 12.2 *Nottingham city centre*

POINTS TO REMEMBER

- Choose only small shops, not big department stores and supermarkets, as it would be hard to survey such a large shop area.
- The time of day and the season will have an effect on which shops are busiest.
- Special events such as spring sales, market day or Christmas shopping may seriously affect your results (Figure 12.3).
- Tourist areas and those around major bus/rail stations might also give high results at certain times.
- 5 minutes may be too short a time period to count pedestrians.

Things to do

1 Why is each shop surveyed several times?

2 What times of day might greatly affect your surveys and why?

3 Why is it impractical to survey department stores on your own?

4 If you had surveyed
   a clothing shops
   b shoe shops
   c hardware stores
   d toy shops
   how might (i) Christmas week and (ii) the spring sales have affected your survey results?

5 Could your results have been affected by the order in which you surveyed the shops?

6 How could you define shop size?

7 a Design a survey to study how the location of shops of different sizes varies in a shopping centre.
   b Where would you expect the largest shops to be found?
   c Draw up a survey sheet to collect these results.
   d What other information might you need to collect in order to help you explain your results?

Figure 12.3 Plan your survey!

Figure 12.4 Survey sheet for a shopping survey

13 *Land use*

> *Subject:* Farming.
>
> *Questions:* Does field size influence land use?
> Does the location of the field cause land use to vary (Figure 13.1)?
>
> *Hypotheses:* The land uses for larger fields will be different from those of smaller ones.
> Land use will be affected by height and aspect (the direction the field faces).

Figure 13.1

WHAT TO MEASURE

You will probably find it difficult to go into each of the fields and measure their area. Field size can be estimated by finding the length of the roadside edges of each field. Alternatively, you could use a map as a secondary data source (Figure 13.2).

Land use is the type of crop or livestock farming that the field is being used for at the time of the survey.

SURVEY DETAILS

Measure the field by pacing, or by using a large tape measure along the roadside edges. Note how the field is being used and any activities that are taking place.

The number of fields that you will be able to survey will depend on the time available.

Comment on the shape of the field, especially if the roadside edges do not give an accurate measure.

From your map, note the height and aspect of the field on your survey sheet.

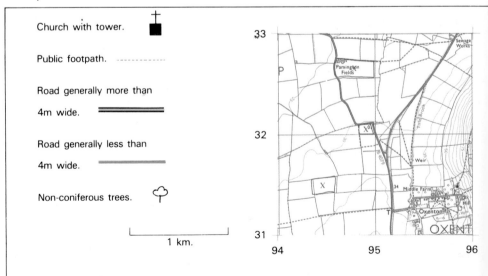

Church with tower.

Public footpath.

Road generally more than 4m wide.

Road generally less than 4m wide.

Non-coniferous trees.

1 km.

Figure 13.2 *Maps can be used as secondary data sources*

POINTS TO REMEMBER

- Ploughed fields are a problem. The survey can really only be done during the growing season when the crops are visible.
- Livestock may not actually be grazing at the times the fields are surveyed. This means you can only class the fields as 'grazing' without being specific.
- Grass is a crop.
- Pacing out distances may not be very accurate.
- Crops might not be easy to recognize. Field sketches and specimens may be useful, or you could ask people living nearby (Figure 13.5).
- Some fields may be used for more than one crop.
- Different land uses within an area may be hard to find. This is because many areas now tend to specialize in only one or two crops (Figure 13.1).
- You will not be surveying fields without a roadside boundary.

Things to do

1 Use the map (Figure 13.2) to calculate the areas of the fields labelled with an 'X'.

2 Why should field size affect a farmer's decision about how to use the land?

3 Why is a winter survey less useful for finding out farming land uses than one carried out in the summer?

4 Land use is a descriptive term. How could you obtain information about land values?

5 List six other factors which may be important in deciding how farmland is used.

6 For one of these factors design a survey to find out if it affects farming land uses.

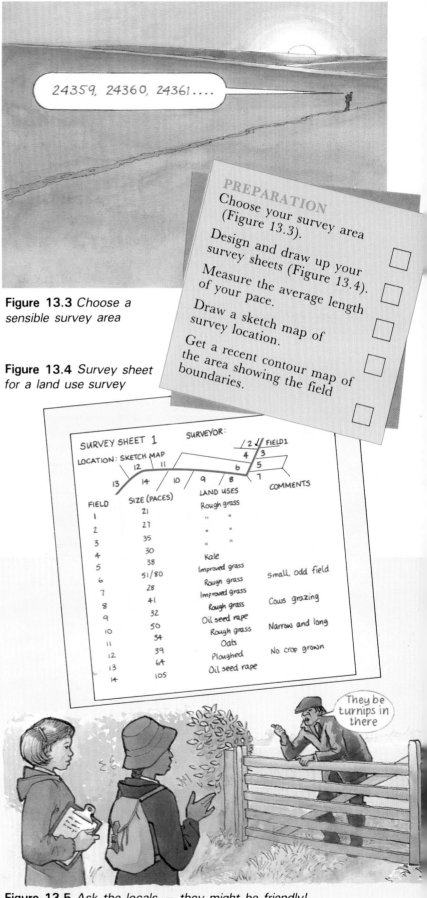

24359, 24360, 24361....

Figure 13.3 *Choose a sensible survey area*

Figure 13.4 *Survey sheet for a land use survey*

PREPARATION

Choose your survey area (Figure 13.3).

Design and draw up your survey sheets (Figure 13.4).

Measure the average length of your pace.

Draw a sketch map of survey location.

Get a recent contour map of the area showing the field boundaries.

SURVEY SHEET 1   SURVEYOR:

FIELD	SIZE (PACES)	LAND USES	COMMENTS
1	21	Rough grass	
2	27	" "	
3	35	" "	
4	30	" "	
5	38	Kale	
6	51/80	Improved grass	Small, odd field
7	28	Rough grass	
8	41	Improved grass	Cows grazing
9	32	Rough grass	
10	50	Oil seed rape	Narrow and long
11	34	Rough grass	
12	39	Oats	
13	64	Ploughed	No crop grown
14	105	Oil seed rape	

They be turnips in there

Figure 13.5 *Ask the locals – they might be friendly!*

Essential services

Subject: Rural services.

Questions: Where do people go to get certain goods and
services (Figure 14.1)?
What factors are important in deciding where
they go?
How important is private transport?

Hypothesis: Services that are needed frequently will be used
locally in the village or in the surrounding area.
People with access to a car will generally travel
further for their services and goods.

WHAT TO MEASURE

In order to test these hypotheses you
need to decide which services and
goods you want to survey. The
services which you could study might
include foods which are bought
frequently, such as bread and milk.
Vital emergency services like a doctor
and a chemist could also be included,
as well as facilities such as a post
office, butcher and bank.

SURVEY DETAILS

You need to carry out a street survey
in the village. Interview people to
find out where they usually get
certain services and goods, the
reasons why they go there and the
type of transport they use.

Survey about 20 people in different
parts of the village.

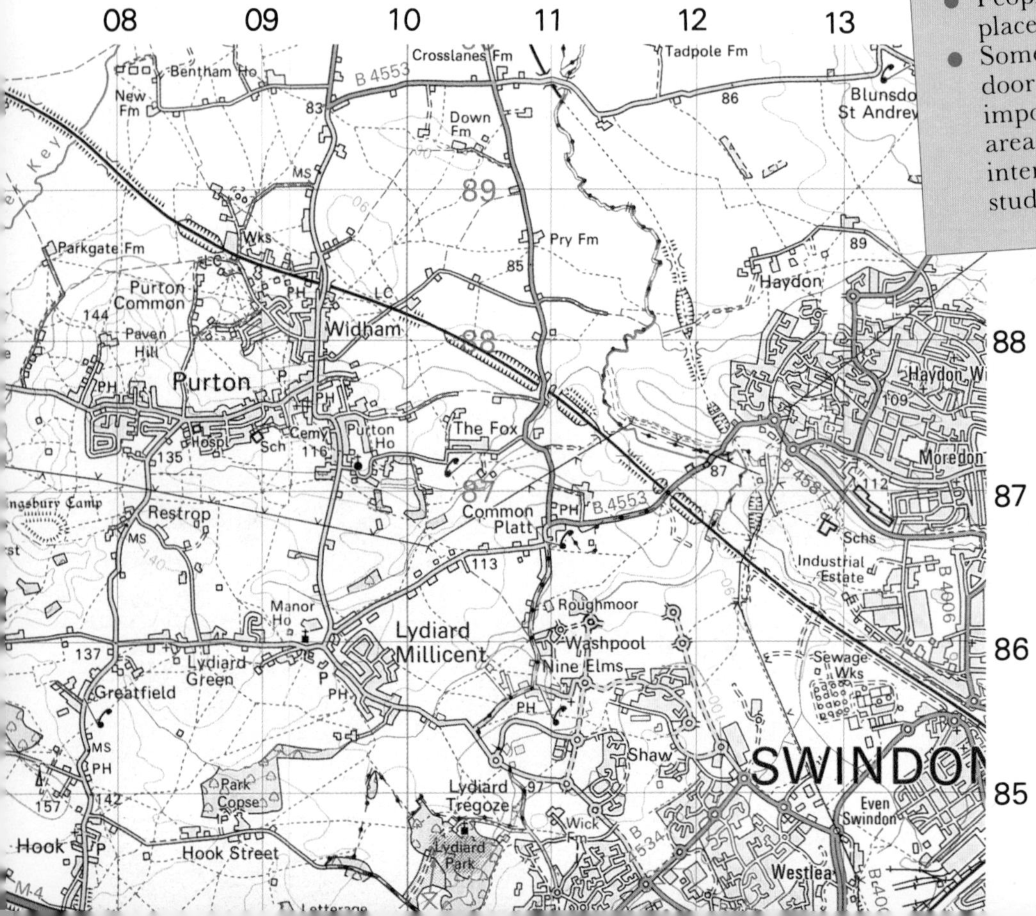

POINTS TO REMEMBER
- The survey will be quite
  lengthy.
- The survey relies on people's
  views and what they
  remember, not what actually
  happens.
- It is difficult to decide which
  services and goods to survey.
  An interesting study might be
  to compare the services in
  different villages.
- People may use a variety of
  places to buy goods.
- Some goods may be delivered
  door-to-door. This is often an
  important service in rural
  areas and could be a very
  interesting part of your
  study.

Figure 14.1

PREPARATION

Choose the village you will survey. ☐

Design and write up your questionnaire (Figure 14.2). ☐

Carry out a trial survey – do your questions work? ☐

Get a detailed map of the village and its surroundings to find out where shops and services are located. ☐

Carry identification. ☐

Things to do

1 Study the map of N.W. Swindon (Figure 14.1). How would you select which village areas to survey? Remember, it is important to get a cross-section of the population.

2 Why has a survey of only 20 people been recommended?

3 What services would you include in your survey?

4 a Suggest where, on Figure 14.1 a family with two children living in Lydiard Millicent (GR 0985), having a car and with both parents working would do
  (i) their daily shopping
  (ii) their weekly shopping.
  b How would a retired couple with no car, living in Purton (GR 085876) differ in their shopping habits?
  c Explain your answers.

5 Look at Figure 14.3. Why do you think this would be a good location to carry out your survey?

6 a Write a list of goods that you would usually expect to be bought in the nearest large town to where you live.
  b Write a hypothesis suggesting which goods will be bought there.
  c Now design a questionnaire to obtain this information.

7 The areas people live in and use are sometimes called 'neighbourhoods'.
  a What might be important in forming such a neighbourhood area?
  b How would you carry out a study to identify neighbourhoods in the area where you live?

DATE	TIME	INTERVIEWED BY:

Excuse me, I'm carrying out a survey for my GCSE Geography, would you mind answering a few questions?

Where do you/your family usually go for these services and give your reasons why.

SERVICE	LOCATION	REASONS/COMMENTS
MILK		
BREAD		
DOCTOR		
DENTIST		
CHEMIST		
BANK		
POST OFFICE		

What other services do you think are essential?

Where do you go for them?

Thank you very much.

Comments: Age 0-15, 16-25, 26-35, 36-45, 46-55, 56+
Male/Female.

Figure 14.2 *Questionnaire for a shopping survey*

Figure 14.3

15 *Soils*

Subject:	Soil surface litter.
Questions:	Are there differences in the amount of soil litter? What reasons account for any differences in soil litter depth?
Hypotheses:	Trees cause the most litter. Soil litter is deepest where trees grow closest together.

Figure 15.1 *Soil surface litter decomposes to form humus*

WHAT TO MEASURE

Soil surface litter is a layer of organic debris which is added to each year by the surrounding vegetation. It is made up of leaves, twigs, branches and other decaying vegetation. This decomposes to form humus. (Figure 15.1)

You can recognize the humus layer as it no longer looks like the debris which it originated from. This is because the litter has been fully decomposed.

The litter depth is measured from the top surface down to the humus, or decomposed, layer.

SURVEY DETAILS

Survey the litter using an ordered sample. Mark out survey points 5 metres apart along a transect, being careful not to disturb the soil litter on one side of this line (Figure 15.2).

Prepare the first site for survey. First, remove all the litter from one side of the survey line. Then, use a ruler to measure litter depth at six points at this site. Repeat the survey every 5 metres along the line (transect).

Survey as many transects as you can across the study area, making sure you disturb the soil litter as little as possible.

Carefully draw a detailed map of the trees, bushes and other features (both natural and built by people) in and just beyond your study area (Figure 15.3). Do this by measuring the distances between the features and using compass bearings.

Figure 15.2 *Soil litter transect survey*

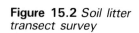
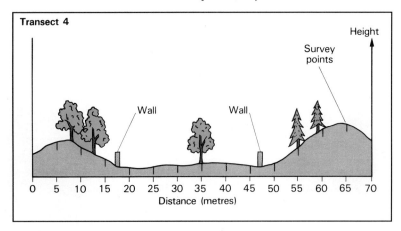

PREPARATION

Select your survey area.

Design and draw up your survey sheets.

Take equipment – ruler, large tape measure and trowel.

Get permission to survey.

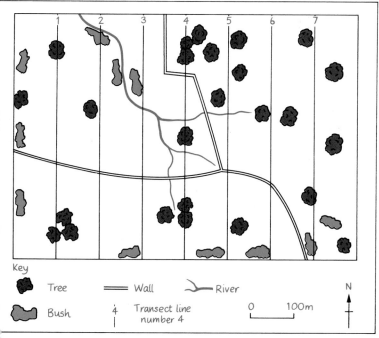

Key
- Tree
- Bush
- Wall
- Transect line number 4
- River
- 0 100m
- N

Figure 15.3 *Sketch map of vegetation*

POINTS TO REMEMBER
- The survey is best done during autumn and winter months. At this time vegetation growth is slow and litter builds up.
- Litter is easily disturbed during the survey (Figure 15.4).
- Work into the wind, surveying upslope if possible to avoid moving litter down the slope as you walk.
- Take into account any artificial and temporary obstacles to litter movement.
- You may find that litter depth is difficult to measure accurately.

Things to do

1 Study Figure 15.5
 a Where does soil litter come from?
 b What determines the supply of litter to a soil?
 c Under what conditions would a soil build up its litter layer?
 d When might a soil be without any litter at all?

2 Why is litter depth measured six times at each site?

3 On a windy day, why should you survey into the wind?

4 Look at Figures 15.2, 15.3 and 15.5. What effects would you expect the wall to have on soil litter?

5 a Make a copy of transect 4 (Figure 15.2).
 b Draw on the transect where you would expect the litter to collect if there was a northerly wind.
 c Write a hypothesis about the amount of soil litter you would expect to find around the walls on transect 4.
 d Draw a sketch graph of your expected results.
 e Draw up a survey sheet that you could use to collect data along transect 4.

Figure 15.4 *Soil litter is easily disturbed*

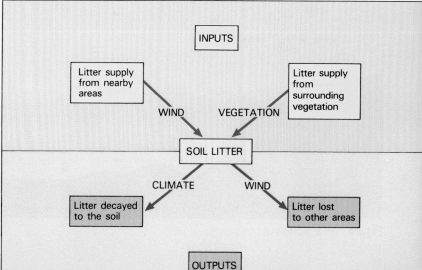

Figure 15.5 *Flow chart: soil litter*

INPUTS

Litter supply from nearby areas

Litter supply from surrounding vegetation

WIND VEGETATION

SOIL LITTER

CLIMATE WIND

Litter decayed to the soil

Litter lost to other areas

OUTPUTS

16 *Vegetation*

Subject: Amount and type of vegetation.

Questions: How does the type and quantity of vegetation alter around a path?
What factors might be important in determining where vegetation doesn't grow?

Hypotheses: The variety of plants and amount of vegetation will increase away from the path (Figure 16.1).
Soil compaction (how compact the soil is) will be greatest nearest the path and decrease further away.
Soil acidity will not vary to any great extent from the path and so it is not an important factor.

WHAT TO MEASURE

To measure the amount of vegetation you need to work out what proportion of the ground has vegetation growing on it.

To measure vegetation type, you could do a detailed survey of all the plant species. Alternatively, you could simplify the survey by looking at how much of the ground has each of the major groups of plants growing on it, such as:
- the ground layer (e.g. mosses)
- the field layer (e.g. grasses)
- the shrub layer
- the tree layer.

Soil compaction is how compressed the soil is. Compacted soils have been squashed, forcing air out of them. To find out the amount of soil compaction, measure the amount of air in the soil.

Figure 16.1

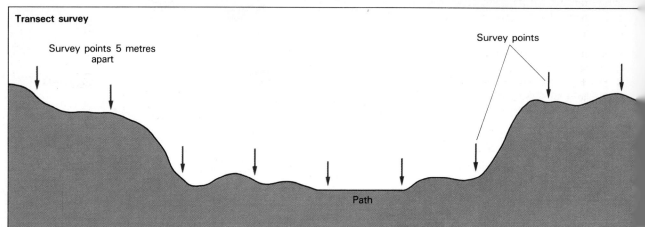

Transect survey

Survey points 5 metres apart

Survey points

Path

Figure 16.2 *Survey sites across a path*

Soil acidity is the hydrogen ion concentration in the soil. It is measured by surveying pH, on a scale from 1 to 13. Values of 1 to 6 are acidic, 7 is neutral. Above a pH of 7 the soil is basic.

SURVEY DETAILS

Prepare a line survey (transect) across the path (Figure 16.2). Survey as many transects as possible, depending on the time you have.

Place a quadrat on the ground (Figure 16.3) and count the number of squares with vegetation growing in them and then the number of different types of plant you see.

Measure soil pH, using a pH meter, in five squares of the quadrat selected at random (Figure 16.4).

Collect a small soil sample by hammering a steel tube into the soil and then removing it. Place this sample in a labelled sample bag.

Repeat the survey every metre along the transect.

Back at school the soil samples need to be removed from the bags, kept separately and dried for 24–48 hours in a warm oven to remove any moisture. Then they need to be weighed. The lower the weight, the greater the air content and the less compacted the soil was.

Things to do

Study Figure 16.5

1 What factors, other than soil properties, affect vegetation growth?

2 What effect might a large tree near the footpath have on:
   a the temperature and amount of sunlight the vegetation gets
   b the amount of vegetation
   c the vegetation height?

3 a Write a hypothesis and devise a survey to investigate what effect the branches of a large tree might have on vegetation.
   b Design and draw up the survey sheet you would use to collect the data.

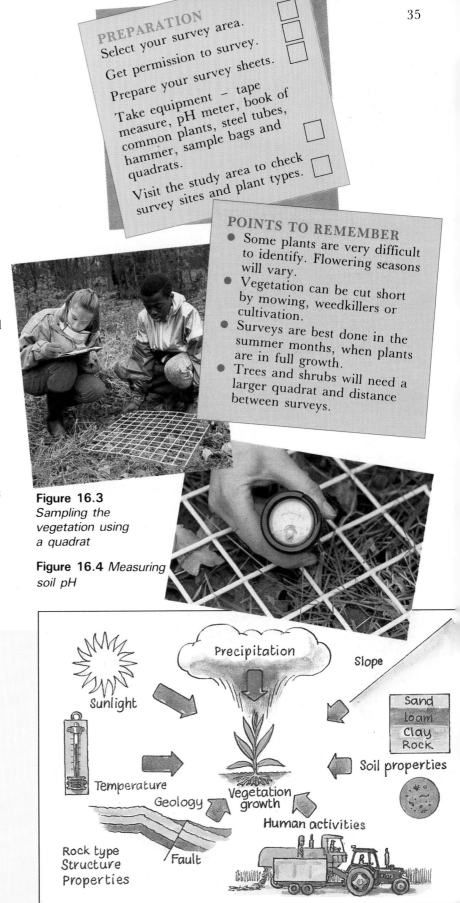

PREPARATION
Select your survey area.
Get permission to survey.
Prepare your survey sheets.
Take equipment – tape measure, pH meter, book of common plants, steel tubes, hammer, sample bags and quadrats.
Visit the study area to check survey sites and plant types.

POINTS TO REMEMBER
- Some plants are very difficult to identify. Flowering seasons will vary.
- Vegetation can be cut short by mowing, weedkillers or cultivation.
- Surveys are best done in the summer months, when plants are in full growth.
- Trees and shrubs will need a larger quadrat and distance between surveys.

Figure 16.3 *Sampling the vegetation using a quadrat*

Figure 16.4 *Measuring soil pH*

Figure 16.5 *Some factors affecting vegetation growth*

Sediment analysis

Subject: Physical geography, sediments.

Questions: What differences are there in sediment size, shape and position in a deposit? What processes may have been involved in their deposition?

Hypotheses: Stones will be angular in shape and sorted by size. The long axes will point in a similar direction and so will the angle of dip. Gravity was the dominant force in the deposition of the sediments.

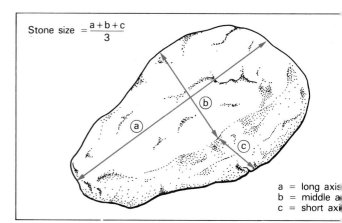

Stone size $= \dfrac{a+b+c}{3}$

a = long axis
b = middle axis
c = short axis

Figure 17.1 *Measuring stone size*

WHAT TO MEASURE

Stone size is measured by finding the average of the long axis (a), the middle axis (b) and the short axis (c) shown in Figure 17.1.

In order to eliminate processes which were probably not important you should also survey the:
- shape (roundness, angularity)
- orientation (direction long axis points)
- dip (angle from the horizontal) of the stones.
A note of the rock type (geology) may also be very useful.

Use Power's roundness scale (Unit 10) to classify the stones in your sample, then use Figure 17.2 to help you identify the possible processes involved.

SURVEY DETAILS

To survey deposits on a slope, you first need to select your stone sample. This is done by gently placing a quadrat on the ground and choosing a stone at random from inside the quadrat.

Without moving the stone, find its longest axis. Use a protractor to measure the dip (angle from the horizontal) of the long axis (Figure 17.3). Then use a compass to measure the direction in which the long axis is pointing.

You can now pick the stone up, without disturbing any others, and measure its size. You should measure a sample of 20 stones at each site. Repeat the survey every 5 metres, moving up the slope.

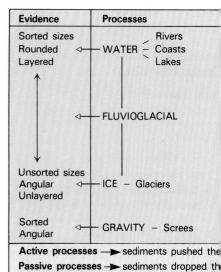

Evidence	Processes
Sorted sizes Rounded ← WATER Layered	Rivers Coasts Lakes
	FLUVIOGLACIAL
Unsorted sizes Angular ← ICE – Glaciers Unlayered	
Sorted Angular ← GRAVITY – Screes	
Active processes → sediments pushed the	
Passive processes → sediments dropped th	
Active processes Dip and orientation show a preference **Passive processes** Dip and orientation not in any preferred direction	

Figure 17.2 *Sediment analysis: identifying processes*

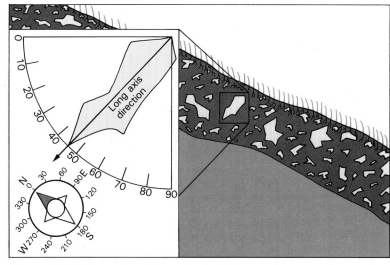

Figure 17.3 *Measuring dip and orientation*

POINTS TO REMEMBER
● The stones may have been
affected artifically, such as by
walls or in building work.
● Steep areas are dangerous
(Figure 17.4).
● Keep away from unstable
slopes.
● Wear suitable clothing and
footwear.
● Make a note of any
landforms you see in the
area.

Shall I survey this stone?

Figure 17.4 *Avoid dangerous sites!*

Things to do

1 Why should the survey sites be
evenly spread?

2 If the stones were larger at the
bottom of the slope and looked
rounded in shape, how do you
think they might have been
deposited?

3 What other evidence of physical
processes would you look for in
and around the survey area?

Look at Figure 17.3
4 Devise a method of measuring the
size of these sediments.

5 Measure the size and angle of dip
of ten of these stones.

6 List your results and those
provided for orientation and
angularity in Figure 17.5.

7 Now refer to Figure 17.2. Which
processes can you eliminate as
being important to their
deposition?

Orientation of stones (from Figure 17.3)		
Stone	Orientation (0° = North)	Angularity
1	141°	very angular
2	72°	very angular
3	107°	very angular
4	270°	very angular
5	14°	sub-angular
6	55°	sub-angular
7	111°	very angular
8	86°	very angular
9	195°	very angular
10	223°	very angular
11	35°	very angular
12	61°	very angular

Figure 17.5 *Stone orientation and angularity*

Flowing water

Subject: Physical geography, streams.
Questions: Where does a stream flow faster? What factors affect water speed?
Hypotheses: Faster flows will occur on the steepest, deepest and smoothest parts of the channel. Gradient and friction are important factors affecting stream speed.

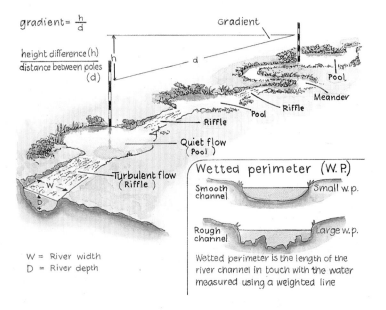

Figure 18.1 *Measuring streams*

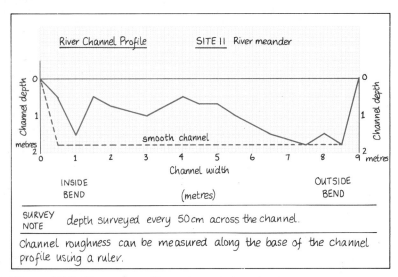

Figure 18.2 *Channel profile and wetted perimeter*

WHAT TO MEASURE

You need to survey gradient, channel shape and river speed (Figure 18.1).

1 GRADIENT

$$\text{gradient} = \frac{\text{height difference (h)}}{\text{distance measured (d)}}$$

2 CHANNEL SHAPE

You can measure this in two ways.
(a) By the width and depth of the stream:

$$\text{shape} = \frac{\text{mean width (w)}}{\text{mean depth (x)}}$$

(b) The wetted perimeter (p). This is how rough or smooth the channel is.

3 WATER SPEED (Figure 18.3)

$$\text{speed} = \frac{\text{distance travelled (d)}}{\text{time taken (t)}}$$

SURVEY DETAILS

Measure out the river length you will survey with a tape measure. Mark each end of the survey site with a range pole (Figure 18.1).

Survey the width of the stream at ten places between the two range poles.

Measure the channel shape. You can do this either by allowing a weighted line to settle on the channel floor, or by drawing the shape of the river channel (Figure 18.2).

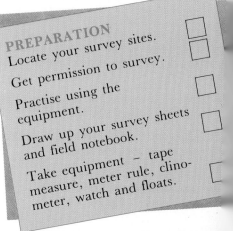

PREPARATION

Locate your survey sites.

Get permission to survey.

Practise using the equipment.

Draw up your survey sheets and field notebook.

Take equipment – tape measure, meter rule, clinometer, watch and floats.

Now measure the gradient using a **clinometer** (Figure 18.3). You should measure the angle six times between each pair of range poles as clinometers can be unreliable.

Water speed is calculated by timing a float (or orange) as it travels between the two range poles (Figure 18.3). Repeat the timing at least six times.

The water speed at the surface has been found to be faster than the mean speed:

mean water speed = 0.85 × surface speed

You could use a flow meter to give a direct reading of water speed.

You need to survey as many sites as possible along the stream.

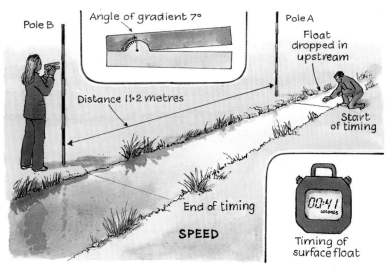

Figure 18.3 *Measuring gradient and water speed*

Things to do

1 In what units is river speed measured?

2 Under what stream conditions might the floats get stuck?

3 How might the river speed be affected by an obstruction, like tree roots, on the river bank?

4 a Measure the length of the channel profile in Figure 18.2.
   b How does your answer compare with the smoother channel shown by the dotted line?

5 a Measure the gradient shown by the clinometer and the time by the stopwatch in Figure 18.3.
   b Estimate the accuracy of the clinometer and the stopwatch.

6 Using the information in Figure 18.3, calculate the surface water speed and estimate the mean water speed.

7 Most river channels are made up of pools and riffles (Figure 18.1). Design a survey to investigate their influence on river speed.

8 Write out your hypothesis and design the survey sheet you would use.

Figure 18.4 *Good fieldwork results in discovery!*

School-based and environmental enquiries

SCHOOL-BASED STUDIES

This section deals with a few ideas involving geographical enquiries in and around school.

IN SCHOOL
Primary data

You could carry out a questionnaire survey of pupils, teachers and workers at school. You might investigate:

- where the busiest areas around your school are
- where people live, to find the catchment area of your school (Figure 19.1)

- the neighbourhoods which people in your school come from and the links between different people in your school.

Other surveys might include:

- a litter survey, which areas of the school are used most? (Figure 19.2)
- how and why the entrances and exits are used during the day.

Secondary data

Schools have pupil records which might provide useful additional information for your enquiry.

Possible studies might include:

- changes in the area served by the school
- pupil numbers and local population changes (using census information), for example age, sex, etc.

Remember that, in most cases, some primary data must be collected in your enquiry.

AROUND THE SCHOOL

A large range of opportunities for enquiries are possible. Much depends on the site and surroundings of your school.

Studies involving the effects of the school buildings on the surroundings could include:

- meteorological studies of temperature and rainfall
- the movements of people in the school grounds
- the perception and image of the school in the surrounding area (Figure 19.3), such as the size of buildings and the perceived distances from various places.

Figure 19.1 *Catchment area of Shaftsbridge School*

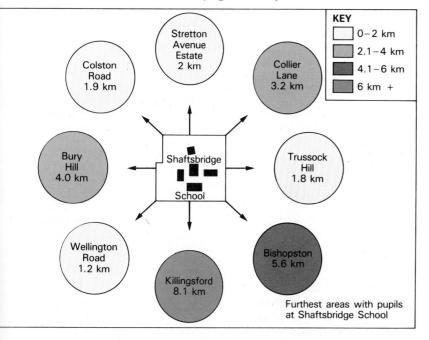

KEY

- 0–2 km
- 2.1–4 km
- 4.1–6 km
- 6 km +

Stretton Avenue Estate 2 km

Colston Road 1.9 km

Collier Lane 3.2 km

Bury Hill 4.0 km

Shaftsbridge School

Trussock Hill 1.8 km

Wellington Road 1.2 km

Killingsford 8.1 km

Bishopston 5.6 km

Furthest areas with pupils at Shaftsbridge School

Figure 19.2 *Litter surveys can be linked to how people use an area*

Things to do

1 Design a survey that you might carry out in or around your school.

2 Draw a sketch map of the area you would survey.

3 Where would you get your information from?

comparison of schools and their
...ation might also make an
...eresting study.

...NVIRONMENTAL
...URVEYS

...bject: Pollution.

...llution happens when foreign
...ostances are added to the
...vironment.

...quiries can study:
* air pollution (Figure 19.4)
* water pollution
* ground pollution
* people's views on pollution.

...me possible studies are outlined in
...s section.

...SUAL IMPACT

...survey of how an area looks is an
...direct way of identifying pollution.
...u could conduct a questionnaire
...rvey of how people are influenced
...ually by their surroundings. Litter,
...affiti and building design might all
... included.

...u might survey the visual pollution
...used by smoke as part of your
...llution survey (Figure 19.4).
...rveys of visibility will take time to
...rry out, but local weather records
...ld give you useful data. The
...ects of local planning controls,
...ch as smokeless zones, might prove
...eresting to study.

...HEMICAL POLLUTION

...rveys of acid rain can be carried
...t. Studies of organisms in streams
...d the effect of chemical pollution
...the plants and wildlife along river
...nks (Figure 19.5) would provide a
...od basis for such an environmental
...vey.

Figure 19.3 *General views on Shaftsbridge School*

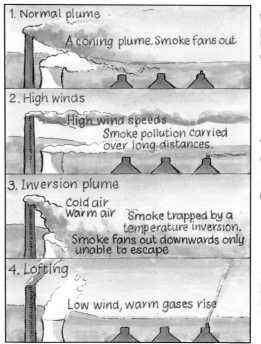

Figure 19.4 *Smoke plumes: smoke drifting downwind varies according to the wind conditions, turbulence and air temperatures*

Valleys can also trap pollutants. Coastal breezes can concentrate smoke pollutants.

You can measure the amount of visibility by picking out land-forms and sites you can see.

The distance the smoke is travelling can also be estimated in this way.

Figure 19.5 *Chemical pollution in streams: a good basis for environmental surveys*

Things to do

Design a survey to carry out one of the investigations suggested on this page.

Draw up the survey sheets you would use.

a Describe how you might carry out an enquiry to investigate how trees affect people's views on the environmental quality of an area near your home.

b Design the questionnaire you would use.

c Draw a sketch map of the area and mark on it the results you would expect to get.

For your own enquiry:
Design a list of things to prepare and points to remember.

20 *Working with figures*

Once you have collected your information, your results have to be presented by sorting and simplifying them. This will involve a number of skills:
- drawing
- plotting
- describing
- sorting and ordering
- designing
- selecting
- organizing.

Your survey results should be presented in both **visual** and **numerical** ways.

TABLES OF RESULTS

Raw data is often too complex for the main points to be drawn from it (Figure 20.1). Your work should contain a summary or simplified version of your results. This must include well organized results tables (Figure 20.2).

Your data may contain too many figures to be easy to follow. You may need to calculate averages (see Unit 30).

Data can also be made simpler by grouping the results together into classes (Figure 20.3).

Tabulated data can be readily graphed and mapped.

Figure 20.1 *Too much data can be as big a problem as too little*

TOWN/VILLAGE NAME	Distance from survey area (Km)	Bus frequency (per day)	Road access 0-9 scale
BRADFORD-ON-AVON	13	45	8
RADSTOCK	12.3	44	6
KEYNSHAM	11.5	43	6
SALTFORD	8.0	43	5
CORSTON	6.0	30	4
TROWBRIDGE	18.5	29	8
BATHEASTON	5.5	27	7
BOX	4.4	22	5
PEASEDOWN	9.0	22	5
PAULTON	13.4	14	3
TIMSBURY	12.0	7	4
RADFORD	9.8	7	3
MARSHFIELD	12.4	3	3
COMBE HAY	7.6	3	4
DYRDAM	10.7	2	2
FRESHFORD	12.1	1	2
FAULKLAND	17.6	1	1

Units clearly stated · Time clearly identified · Well labelled headings · Boxes large enough to record data clearly · All results filled in · Data sorted by bus frequency

Figure 20.2 *Tabulating data*

Shoppers at the local supermarket

Frequent shoppers

Shop regularly · Shop rarely

Stone sizes

Very large stones · Large stones · Medium sized stones

Small stones · Very small stones

Figure 20.3 *Classes of data*

PRIMARY AND SECONDARY DATA SOURCES

Presenting your results can involve using other sources of information.

Results collected by you in the field are called **primary** data. There are many other places to collect valuable information for your enquiry. These are **secondary** data sources (Figure 20.4). They have been collected by someone else. You will need to extract the information you need for your enquiry from the secondary data.

Examples of secondary data sources include:
- bus/rail timetables
- Yellow Pages/trade directories
- tourist guides/maps/plans
- postcards/newspapers/magazines
- census figures
- reports/other documents.

Most of these can be obtained easily. Don't forget that your local library may have lots of helpful sources of information.

SUMMARIES

You must provide a clear statement of the main findings of your fieldwork.

A few questions you may need to answer when summarizing your results are:
- What were the highest values?
- What were the lowest?
- When did they occur?
- Where did they happen?
- Where was the greatest concentration of results?
- Were there any special results?

Figure 20.4 *Some secondary data sources*

Things to do

1 Simplify the stone size data shown in Figure 20.3 by grouping the figures into three classes.

2 Look at Figure 20.5
   a Prepare a table that you could use to show this type of information.
   b Tabulate the data.
   c If you were summarizing the information from this survey sheet, what points would you make?

3 Make a list of the skills you have used in answering these questions.

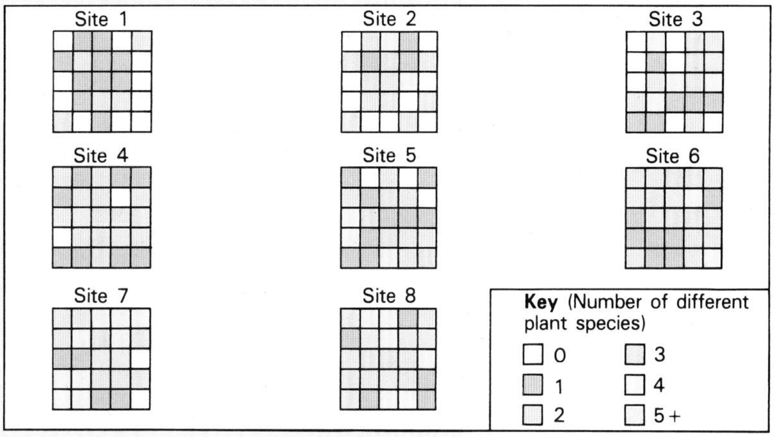

Figure 20.5 *Survey sheet: plant species data*

Site 1 · Site 2 · Site 3 · Site 4 · Site 5 · Site 6 · Site 7 · Site 8

Key (Number of different plant species)
0 1 2 3 4 5+

21 Map skills

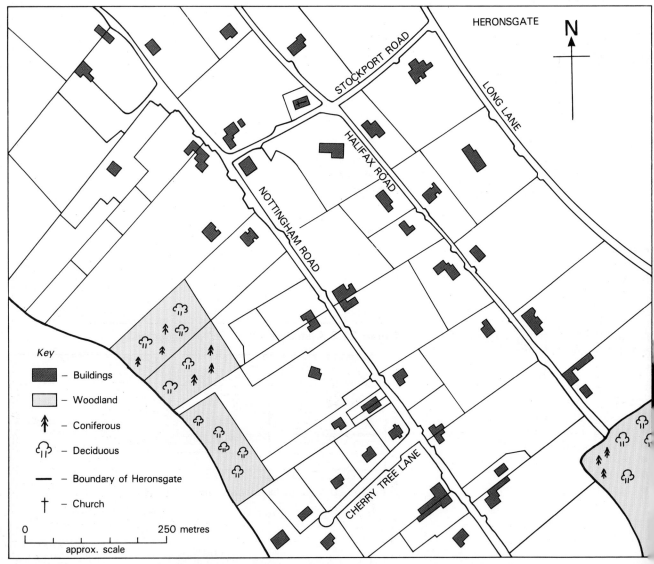

Figure 21.1 *A base map*

DRAWING MAPS

A map is an overhead, visual picture of an area. It uses symbols to describe the area. A base map is a base outline of your study area.

Base maps (Figure 21.1) are useful in your enquiry as they can be used to map selected information. Maps help you to identify your study area and its surroundings.

You can:
● draw or trace base maps from a professionally drawn map
● draw base maps from your own surveys
● leave out any details that you consider unnecessary for your survey.
● change the scale of your base map to fit your survey results.

MAP INTERPRETATION

Some concepts used in map interpretation are:

distance	direction
area	slope
site	situation
function	location

EOGRAPHERS SHOULD RAW AND USE MAPS!

ps are:
used to locate places
used for comparing areas
valuable for plotting data
used for drawing plans.

ENERAL STRUCTIONS

ps are drawn for a particular ject or theme. Some types of map ful in coursework enquiries are:
sketch maps (Unit 22)
dots and spheres (Unit 22)
choropleth maps (Unit 23)
isopleth maps (Unit 24).

OINTS TO REMEMBER

When drawing maps:
- Keep your map simple.
- Make the main point of your map stand out and easy to spot.
- Avoid putting on too much information.
- Mark on and highlight the key features.
- Draw the map accurately and neatly.
- Use a border.
- Give your map a title.
- Use abbreviations and a key.
- Print any labels.

Things to do

From this Unit, write a checklist for drawing base maps. Which points on your list have not been included on the student's map in Figure 21.2?

Study the map drawn in Figure 21.3. Write a list of things which you think need to be done to improve it.

Redraw Figure 21.3 to show the information more clearly.

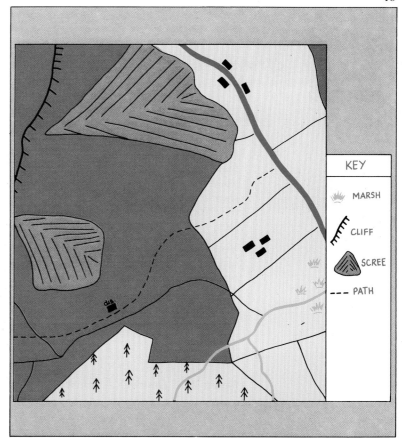

Figure 21.2 *A student's map. What's missing?*

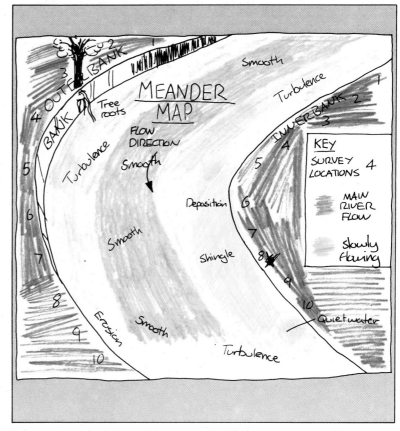

Figure 21.3 *A student's map. How could it be improved?*

22 Sketch maps

A sketch map is a drawing of your study area. It can be estimated or measured. You should plot the main features and the relative locations of your survey points. Your sketch map should give a simple visual description of what is at and around each survey site (Figure 22.1).

You must always draw sketch maps of your survey sites. Sketch maps will usually help you understand the results you obtain. Sketch maps should form an important part of your field notebook.

HOW TO DRAW A SKETCH MAP

In the field, sketch maps can be drawn without any complex equipment. This is how to draw one:
● mark the corners of your map
● measure (or pace) the distance between the corners
● identify any features you want to include
● measure the distance and bearing of each feature from the nearest corner
● label these measurements in pencil on your map
● redraw your map accurately after fieldwork
● add any special notes
● label the map clearly and construct a key.

Major natural and artificial features should be mapped. These may include slopes, landforms, buildings or even trees.

Figure 22.1 *Drawing a sketch map*

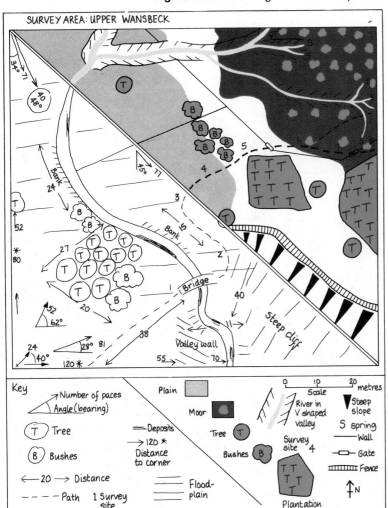

Things to do

1 Draw a sketch map of the area around your classroom. Clearly label the main entrances and exits. Add labels for any other points of interest.

2 a From the OS map (Figure 22.2), draw a sketch map of the location of the village of Axbridge.
   b Label on your map why you think Axbridge has not expanded to the south.
   c Add these labels to your map:
      i. steep scarp
      ii. gap
      iii. river flood plain
      iv. permeable rocks
      v. gentle slopes.
   d If Axbridge grew in size over the next 10 years, draw clearly on your sketch map where you would expect it to grow. Explain your reasons for choosing these sites for expansion.

DOT MAPS

Dot maps (Figure 22.3) are used to plot position or locations. They show where things are and any patterns which result. Dot maps allow these patterns to be analysed (see Unit 36).

Dots of different sizes and colours can be used.

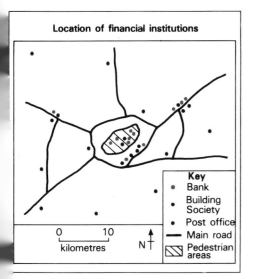

Figure 22.3 *A dot map*

Figure 22.4 *Using shapes: mean traffic flows through Winstanton Trading Estate*

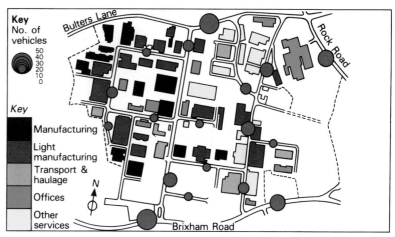

SPHERES AND SHAPES

The sizes of the numbers in your results from different survey areas can be mapped using different sized shapes. The larger the shape, the bigger the number (Figure 22.4). Make sure that the big shapes do not cover and hide the smaller ones.

In a similar way, you can draw pictograms of your results, where the picture relates directly to what you measured (Figure 22.5).

Figure 22.5 *A pictogram*

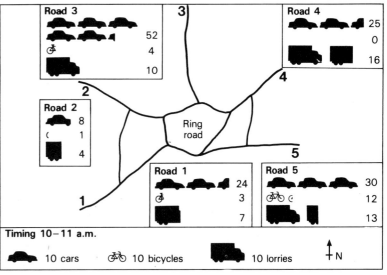

Choropleth maps

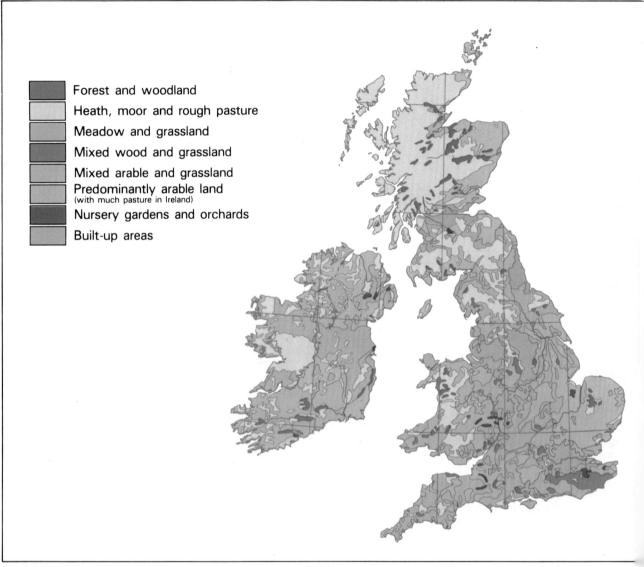

Forest and woodland
Heath, moor and rough pasture
Meadow and grassland
Mixed wood and grassland
Mixed arable and grassland
Predominantly arable land
(with much pasture in Ireland)
Nursery gardens and orchards
Built-up areas

Figure 23.1

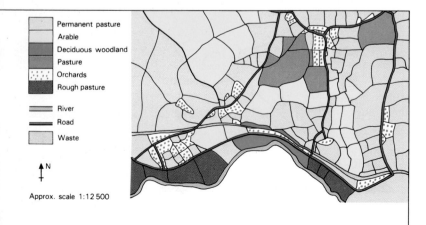

Permanent pasture
Arable
Deciduous woodland
Pasture
Orchards
Rough pasture
River
Road
Waste

N

Approx. scale 1:12 500

A choropleth map is a map which has been shaded. This type of map i used when data has been collected fc areas with boundaries such as political or administrative areas or land use boundaries (Figures 23.1 and 23.2).

Figure 23.2 *Choropleth map of agricultural land use*

When drawing choropleth maps (Figure 23.3), if you want to show the higher results most clearly, use darker or deeper shading for them. If the lower results are most important, use the darker colours and shades for these.

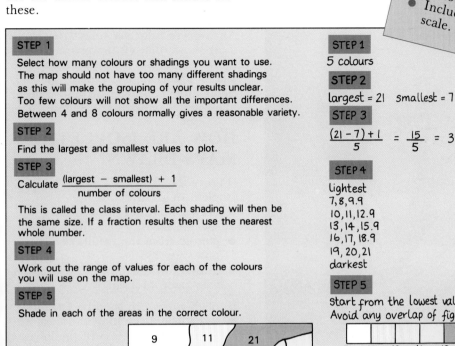

STEP 1

Select how many colours or shadings you want to use. The map should not have too many different shadings as this will make the grouping of your results unclear. Too few colours will not show all the important differences. Between 4 and 8 colours normally gives a reasonable variety.

STEP 2

Find the largest and smallest values to plot.

STEP 3

Calculate $\dfrac{(\text{largest} - \text{smallest}) + 1}{\text{number of colours}}$

This is called the class interval. Each shading will then be the same size. If a fraction results then use the nearest whole number.

STEP 4

Work out the range of values for each of the colours you will use on the map.

STEP 5

Shade in each of the areas in the correct colour.

STEP 1

5 colours

STEP 2

largest = 21   smallest = 7

STEP 3

$\dfrac{(21 - 7) + 1}{5} = \dfrac{15}{5} = 3$

STEP 4

lightest
7, 8, 9.9
10, 11, 12.9
13, 14, 15.9
16, 17, 18.9
19, 20, 21
darkest

STEP 5

Start from the lowest value and work upwards. Avoid any overlap of figures.

7 10 13 16 19 21

Figure 23.3 *Worked example: choropleth maps*

Things to do

Figure 23.4 shows a map with data obtained during a study of Norwich about people's views on local shopping facilities.

1 Make a tracing of the base map of Norwich (Figure 23.4).

2 **a** Select the number of colours or shadings you want to use.
   b Calculate the class interval.
   c Prepare and draw your key.
   d Draw a choropleth map of the data for Norwich on your base map.

From your map:

3 **a** Where are the highest values located?
   b Which parts have the lowest values?

4 Suggest possible reasons for your answers to question 3.

5 Why is this map not useful for giving information about streets?

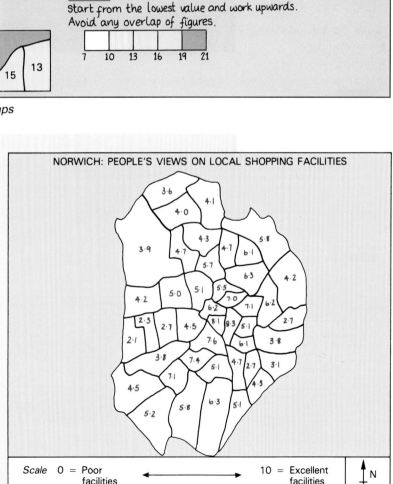

NORWICH: PEOPLE'S VIEWS ON LOCAL SHOPPING FACILITIES

Scale 0 = Poor facilities   10 = Excellent facilities   ↑ N

Figure 23.4 *Base map of Norwich: views on local shopping facilities*

24 Isopleth maps

Figure 24.1 *Isopleth maps are widely used*

An isopleth map has lines drawn on it. It shows that all the places joined by the same line have the same value. These maps are used frequently. Examples include contour maps and weather maps (Figure 24.1).

HOW ARE ISOPLETH MAPS DRAWN?

(Figure 24.2)

Isopleth maps are:
- drawn from data collected at specific points
- plotted from the results of any point surveys
- drawn to show how survey results vary over an area.

Isopleth maps can then be used to:
- show where the highest values are
- identify the location of the lowest point
- locate easily the places of greatest variation
- mark places which have little variety.

POINTS TO REMEMBER
- Start by drawing in pencil, as it is easy to make mistakes (Figure 24.3). You can ink the lines in later.
- Label each line clearly on the line.
- Check that the lines don't change in value by more than the interval you have chosen.
- Lines cannot cross one another.
- Don't use a ruler to join up the points.
- Estimate the position of the line between the points. Decide which points it should be closer to, and draw it in.
- Point surveys may miss out some places.

STEP 1

Plot your results as points on a map.

STEP 2

Now find the lowest and highest values on the map. On this map the lowest value is 12 and the highest is 66. Next, decide what interval you want to have between the lines and how many lines between your highest and lowest values.
It may be helpful to follow the rhyme: 'Not too many and not too few. Four to eight will probably do!'
In this example, if lines were drawn for 20, 30, 40, 50 and 60 that would make 5 in all with an interval of 10 between each line.

STEP 3

The first line to draw is the one above the lowest number. In this case, 12 was the smallest and 20 would be the first line to draw as no points on the map lie below 10. Carefully draw, in pencil, the first line, say 20 in this example. Then follow with the next (30) and so on, until the highest number is reached.

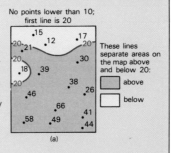

No points lower than 10; first line is 20

These lines separate areas on the map above and below 20:
- ▓ above
- ☐ below

(a)

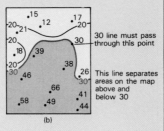

30 line must pass through this point

This line separates areas on the map above and below 30

(b)

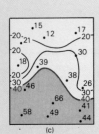

(c)

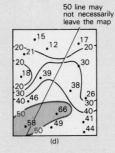

50 line may not necessarily leave the map

(d)

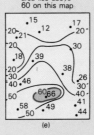

Only one small area lies above 60 on this map

(e)

Figure 24.2 *Worked example: isopleth maps*

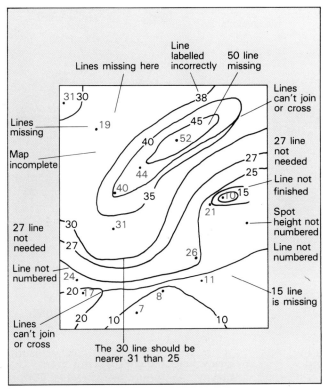

Figure 24.3 *Isopleth maps: some likely mistakes*

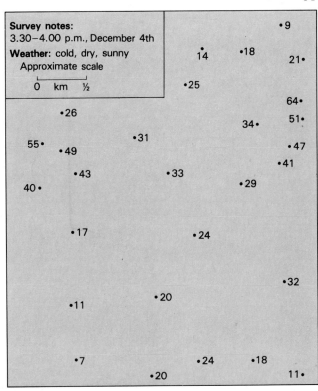

Figure 24.4 *Pedestrian numbers in central Bath*

Things to do

1 Make a tracing of Figure 24.4. This is a map of the number of pedestrians in the central area of Bath, counted at 3.30 p.m. on a winter's day.

2 **a** Find the lowest and highest values and decide how many lines you want to use.
  b Work out what interval you want to use between the lines and which line to draw first.
  c Draw an isopleth map of the numbers of pedestrians in Bath.

3 **a** Where are the lines closest together?
  b What does this show?

4 **a** On your map, label the area with the lowest pedestrian numbers.
  b Suggest why there might be so few pedestrians here.

5 Study Figure 24.5. Label on your isopleth map where you expect the busiest pedestrian areas to be at:
  a 18.00 hours (6 p.m.) on this day
  b 15.00 hours (3 p.m.) in summer.
  What reasons are there for your choices?

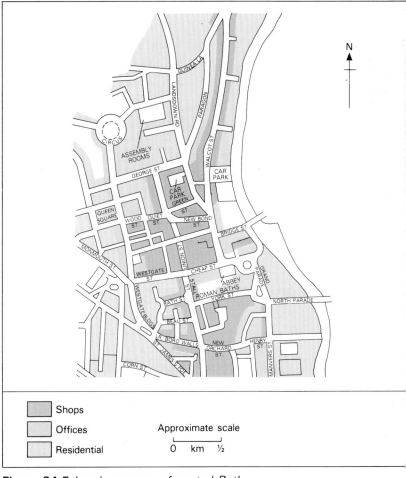

Figure 24.5 *Land use map of central Bath*

25 Sketches

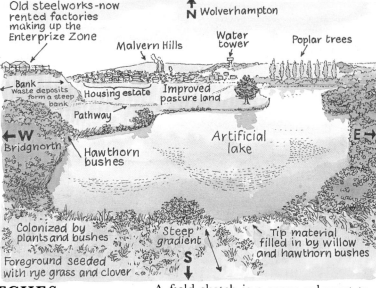

Figure 25.1
Good field sketches can be drawn of fields!

Labels in figure: Old steelworks-now rented factories making up the Enterprize Zone; N Wolverhampton; Malvern Hills; Water tower; Poplar trees; Bank waste deposits form a steep bank; Housing estate; Improved pasture land; ←W Bridgnorth; Pathway; Artificial lake; E→; Hawthorn bushes; Colonized by plants and bushes; Steep gradient; S; Tip material filled in by willow and hawthorn bushes; Foreground seeded with rye grass and clover

FIELD SKETCHES

A field sketch describes the area which you are surveying (Figure 25.1). A sketch helps you to understand your results. It also reminds you of the conditions in which you carried out your survey. Sketches add vital pieces of information to your survey. Field sketches are important to your study, even though they are not detailed.

A field sketch is a scene relevant to your study, including physical or human factors, or both. It is a drawing of your survey site which must be well labelled and have a title.

Draw field sketches during your survey. Annotate any sketches with useful labels. Draw a neat copy of your field sketch when you write up your enquiry.

Some skills involved are:
- observation
- estimation
- visual appraisal
- drawing and sketching
- understanding the landscape.

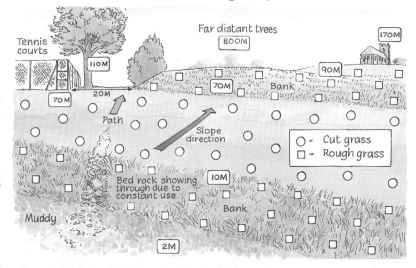

Labels in figure: Tennis courts; Far distant trees 800M; 170M; 110M; 90M; 70M; Bank; 20M; Path; Slope direction; ○ = Cut grass; □ = Rough grass; Bed rock showing through due to constant use; 10M; Bank; Muddy; 2M

Figure 25.2 *A field sketch. What's missing?*

Things to do

Look at the field sketch shown in Figure 25.2.

1 What subjects has the field sketch concentrated on?

2 What major points does the field sketch make?

3 Write a list of surveys for which this field sketch could have been drawn.

SKETCH PROFILES

A profile is a cross-section or slice of the landscape. It is drawn in two dimensions. You can draw profiles for all types of study. Urban profiles (Figure 25.3) are often used in land use studies. Valley profiles (Figure 25.4) can help in understanding physical and human processes.

Figure 25.3 *An urban transect*

Labels in figure: Building height; Central area; High-rise office development; Wilcox St.; Semi-detached housing; Large chain store; James St.; Small shops; Distance from the centre

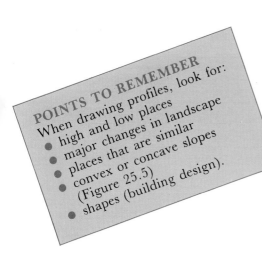

POINTS TO REMEMBER
When drawing profiles, look for:
- high and low places
- major changes in landscape
- places that are similar
- convex or concave slopes (Figure 25.5)
- shapes (building design).

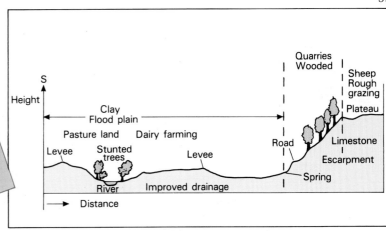

Figure 25.4 *Part of a valley profile*

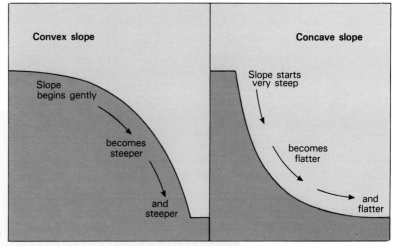

Figure 25.5 *Convex and concave slopes*

Things to do

Study the photograph of a valley in an upland area (Figure 25.6).

1 Draw a sketch profile across the valley to show the changes in height and slope.

2 Look at Figure 25.5 and then label your profile clearly with the following terms:
    steep slope
    convex slope
    concave slope
    flat valley floor.

3 Add other labels for any major landforms you can see in the photograph.

4 What types of survey might your profile be used for?

5 Use the evidence from your sketch profile to describe how you think this valley could have been formed.

6 a Draw a field sketch of the way the land is being used in the valley shown in Figure 25.6.
  b Draw a field sketch of the different types of vegetation shown in Figure 25.6.
  c Compare the two field sketches you have drawn. What differences are there in the drawings and the labels you have used?

Figure 25.6 *Looking down the Nant Ffrancon valley from the lip of Cwm Idwal*

26 *Plotting graphs*

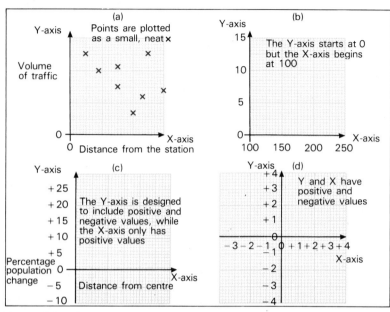

Figure 26.1 *Drawing graphs: getting your axes right*

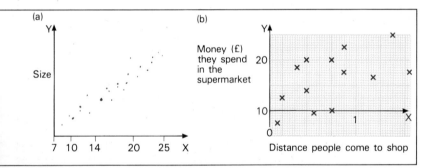

Figure 26.2 *Two scattergraphs*

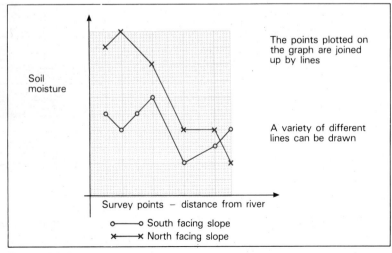

Figure 26.3 *A line graph*

Graphs are usually drawn using special squared paper (Figure 26.1a). Most graphs have two axes, a vertical Y-axis and a horizontal X-axis.

You do not need to start the axes at O (Figure 26.1b). The axes may need to be drawn to include positive and negative values (Figures 26.1c and d).

TO PLOT A GRAPH

- You should normally plot time and distance on the X-axis.
- Size and frequency are plotted on the Y-axis.
- Find the highest and lowest values of X and Y.
- Scale the graph axes so that you can plot all the points on the graph.
- Are there any negative values?
- Do you want the axes to start at O?
- Label the axes clearly (include the units).
- Plot each point on the graph (each point will have a value of X and Y).
- Fill in any curves or lines in pencil first.
- Write a title for the graph.

WHAT GRAPHS COULD BE DRAWN?

GCSE syllabuses ask you to present your data in a variety of ways. There are many types of graph that can be used to draw up your survey results but they may not all be useful for your data.

The types of graph include:
- scattergraphs (Figure 26.2)
- line graphs (Figure 26.3)
- frequency graphs (Figure 26.4)
- kite diagrams (Figure 26.5)
- bar graphs (Unit 27)
- bar charts (Unit 27)
- triangular graphs (Unit 28)
- circular graphs (Unit 28)
- star graphs (Unit 28).

OTHER GRAPH SCALES

If your results contain both very small numbers and large ones then a logarithmic scale can be helpful. This is because it expands the amount of space on the graph paper allowed for small numbers and reduces the space for large ones. A log scale reduces the clustering of points at the lower end of the graph.

For this type of graph you need to use special logarithmic graph paper. Both axes can be logged or just one depending on the data you are plotting.

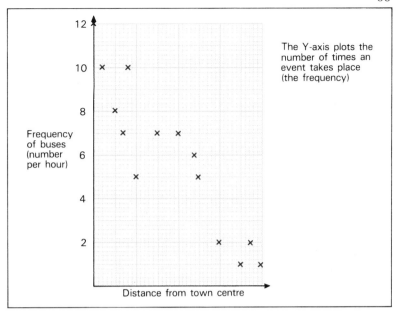

Figure 26.4 *A frequency graph*

Things to do

1 Look at the two graphs shown in Figure 26.2. For each graph, write a list of things that you think should be done to improve it.

2 **a** Write a list of the different types of graph.
  b How is the data presented in the ones shown in this Unit?
  c Make a list of the graphs which plot special types of data. Explain what they are used for.

3 *Survey notes:*
Temperatures measured 1 metre above the ground.
Weather: clear, sunny, calm
Date: 9 December

Look carefully at the information given in Figure 26.6.

  a Decide what type of graph you will draw to plot this data.
  b Decide what you will plot on the X- and Y-axes, then draw and scale these axes.
  c Plot how air temperatures of the east facing slope (Y1) and the south facing one (Y2) vary with distance from the school buildings.
  d What does your graph show you about the temperatures on these slopes as you go further away from the buildings?
  e Which slope had the higher temperatures?
  f Label and title the graph.

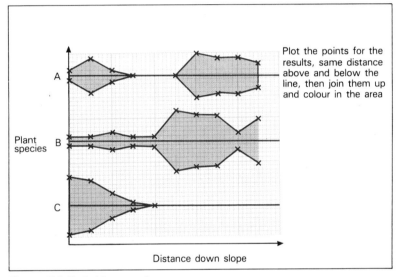

Figure 26.5 *A kite graph*

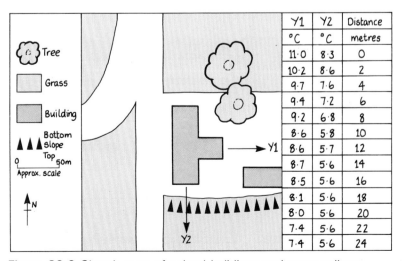

Figure 26.6 *Sketch map of school buildings and surroundings*

27 *Drawing bars*

Bar charts and bar graphs are drawn in a similar way. They have lines or bars drawn on a graph which show the size or the frequency of information. Bar charts and bar graphs can appear in a variety of types and styles for different uses (Figure 27.3).

Figure 27.1 *A bar graph*

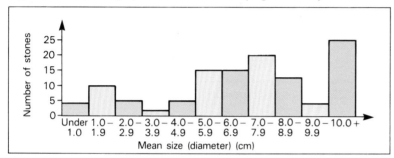

Figure 27.2 *A bar chart*

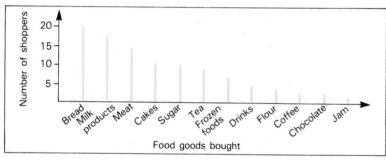

Things to do

1 Look carefully at the bar graph and bar chart drawn in Figures 27.1 and 27.2. Make a list of the differences between the two methods of plotting results in terms of:
   a graph design
   b the results shown and how they are organized
   c the information on the X-axis.

2 Look at the sketch map of land use (Figure 27.4).
   a Draw a table to show how often each type of land use occurs.
   b Count the number of times each land use has been labelled on the map and fill in your table.
   c Decide whether you will draw a bar chart or bar graph and then plot the data from your table.
   d Which graph would you draw to compare two different streets?

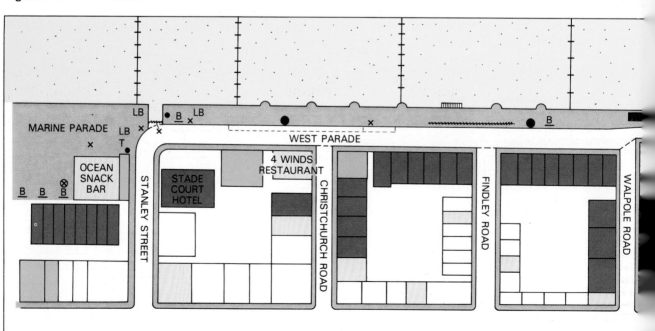

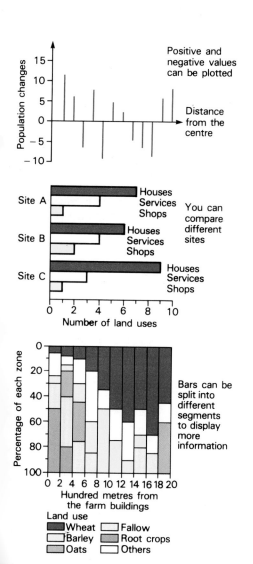

Figure 27.3 Bar graphs and bar charts can be used in different ways

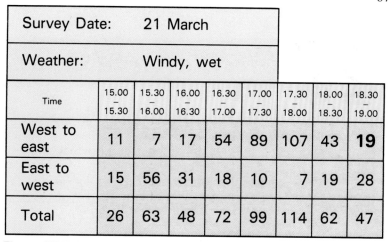

Time	15.00–15.30	15.30–16.00	16.00–16.30	16.30–17.00	17.00–17.30	17.30–18.00	18.00–18.30	18.30–19.00
West to east	11	7	17	54	89	107	43	**19**
East to west	15	56	31	18	10	7	19	28
Total	26	63	48	72	99	114	62	47

Survey Date: 21 March. Weather: Windy, wet

Figure 27.5 Vehicle flows along West Parade

Things to do

1 Look at the sketch map (Figure 27.4) and the table of vehicle flows (Figure 27.5).
a Draw bars to plot vehicle flows along West Parade.
b Label your graph to show when the highest and lowest vehicle flows were.
c Sketch a graph of the traffic situation you might expect between 7 and 9 a.m. along West Parade.
d Label your sketch graph to explain what you think might happen.

Figure 27.4 Sketch map of land use

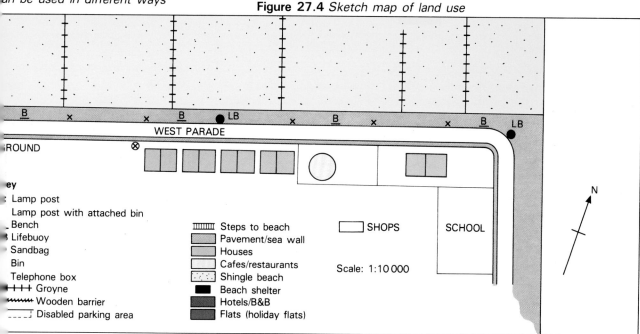

28 *Circular and triangular graphs*

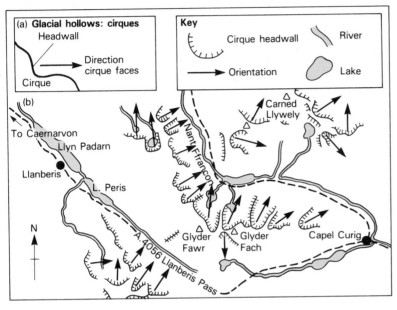

(a) Glacial hollows: cirques
- Headwall
- Direction cirque faces
- Cirque

Key
- Cirque headwall
- Orientation
- River
- Lake

(b)
To Caernarvon
Llyn Padarn
Llanberis
L. Peris
Nant Ffrancon
Carned Llywely
Glyder Fawr
Glyder Fach
Capel Curig
A 4056 Llanberis Pass
N

CIRCULAR GRAPHS

A circular graph is sometimes called a rose diagram. It is used when compass direction or orientation is plotted. For example, you can use it to show the direction people travel.

Circular graphs can also be used to show aspect, or the direction that a slope faces. In Figure 28.1 the direction that mountain hollows or cirques face has been plotted on the sketch map, for a valley in North Wales.

Figure 28.2 shows you how to draw a circular graph.

Figure 28.1 *The orientation of cirques in a valley in North Wales*

STEP 1
The raw data.

STEP 2
Calculate the size of each segment.
- Decide how many segments you want to plot.
- Remember that a number which divides easily into 360 will make the calculations easier. A full circle is 360 degrees.
- Calculate the size of each segment. Divide 360 by the number of segments.

STEP 3
Prepare a table to show the angles in each segment. Count how many times each segment occurs in the raw data, filling in the frequency column of the table.

STEP 4
Prepare your circular graph:
- draw a circle
- divide the circle into the segments you chose in Step 3

Each segment = 40° angle

- draw a scale on the axes of the circular graph
- check that you can plot all the data
- draw the frequency of each segment on the circular graph

Frequency of each segment plotted

- complete the graph by shading in all the segments
- label and title the graph.

Prevailing wind

Wind rose (January 1–22)

Winds mainly from the NNW and NE sectors

STEP 1
Wind direction:
355, 334, 33, 60, 92, 25, 358, 11, 254, 206, 155, 327, 359, 101, 45, 56, 234, 76, 351, 275, 24, 345

STEP 2
9 in this case
segment size = $\frac{360}{9}$ = 40 degrees

STEP 3

Angle	Frequency
0–40	4
41–80	5
81–120	2
121–160	1
161–200	0
201–240	1
241–280	2
281–320	0
321–360	7

Things to do

Look at the sketch map in Figure 28.1b.
1 a Use a protractor to work out which direction each cirque is facing. Use the arrows on the sketch map to help you.
  b Decide how many segments you want to plot and draw a table of how many cirques face each direction.
  c Construct a circular graph for the cirques.

2 a Which direction do the cirques tend to face?
  b Label this clearly on your circular graph.

3 What might your answer to question 2a suggest about these cirques?

4 Why might the opposite side of the valley have no cirques at all?

Figure 28.2 *Worked example: circular graphs*

RIANGULAR GRAPHS

angular graphs have three axes,
X-axis, a Y-axis and a Z-axis.
ey are drawn from an equilateral
angle – a triangle with equal
gth sides. Triangular graphs are
d to plot three sets of data as they
ve three axes (X, Y and Z). The
ee sets of data used (X, Y and Z
ues) must each add up to the same
ue, for example 100 per cent
gure 28.3).

ne uses of triangular graphs
lude:
Comparing the types of industry
in different areas. The location of
points on a triangular graph shows
whether primary, secondary or
tertiary industry dominates and
how different areas compare
(Figure 28.4).
To show sediment size or soil
texture (Figure 28.5).
aphs with more than three axes
also be drawn. These are called
diagrams (Figure 28.6).

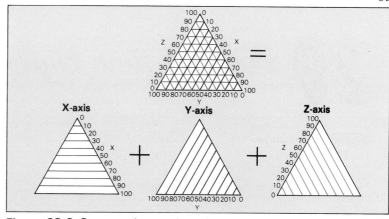

Figure 28.3 *Constructing a triangular graph*

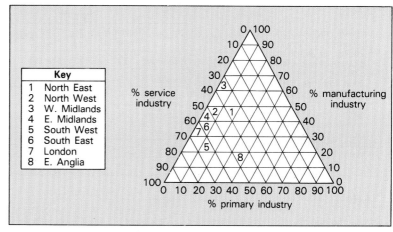

Figure 28.4 *Triangular graph of employment*

Things to do

What are the values of X, Y and
Z for point A in Figure 28.5?

What does Figure 28.5 show
about the soil texture plotted at
points B and C?

Where would a completely mixed
sediment load (equal parts of
sand, silt and clay) be found on
this graph?

a Draw an equilateral triangle and
  the axes for a triangular graph.
b Label the axes X, Y and Z.
c Plot the following figures onto
  it:

	X	Y	Z
site 1	61	25	14
site 2	26	66	8
site 3	14	33	53
site 4	19	31	50
site 5	11	14	75
site 6	8	40	52
site 7	12	30	58
site 8	31	45	24

where X is the percentage of
  rounded stones
  Y is the percentage of
  sub-angular stones
  Z is the percentage of
  angular stones
  at each site.

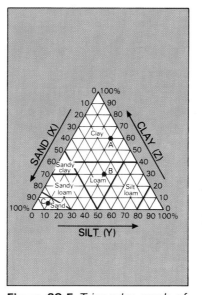

Figure 28.5 *Triangular graph of soil texture*

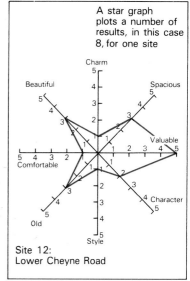

Figure 28.6 *A star diagram*

d From the graph you have
  drawn, put the sites into groups
  which have similar stone
  shapes and write a list of the
  groups.

29 *Pie and flow charts*

PIE CHARTS

Pie charts show proportions. They are diagrams drawn as circles divided into slices or segments. The size of each slice shows how large or small the figure plotted is (Figure 29.1).

SOME SKILLS INVOLVED
- calculating
- measuring
- drawing
- comparing

Things to do

1 **a** Prepare a pie chart and calculate the angles for the data in Figure 29.2.
   b Construct the pie chart for these figures.
   c Give your chart a title and construct a key.

2 What does your pie chart show?

3 Explain why, if you add the angles together, they don't quite total up to 360 degrees.

STEP 1

Prepare your pie chart by:
- drawing a circle and marking the centre point
- drawing a start line for the first slice, from the centre point to the circle.

STEP 2

Calculate the angles for each segment of the pie chart by:
- adding up all the numbers to be plotted (this is the total)
- dividing the first number by this total and then multiplying the result by 360 to get the first angle
- repeating this calculation for each of the proportions.

You will find it useful to check that together the angles add up to 360 degrees. Fractions may sometimes prevent this from happening.

STEP 3

Draw the pie chart:
- measure the first angle from the start line using a protractor and draw the next line
- start from the new line and repeat this operation until all the segments have been marked out.

STEP 4

Colour or shade in each segment. Label each segment, or else use a key.

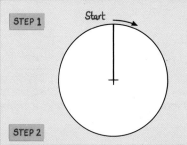

Place	Number of shoppers (N)	$\frac{N}{total}$	$\frac{N}{total} \times 360°$
Bromsgrove	28	$\frac{28}{72}$	140°
Worcester	4	$\frac{4}{72}$	20°
Redditch	6	$\frac{6}{72}$	30°
Halesowen	4	$\frac{4}{72}$	20°
Droitwich	10	$\frac{10}{72}$	50°
Birmingham	20	$\frac{20}{72}$	100°
Total	72		360°

STEP 4 Finished version

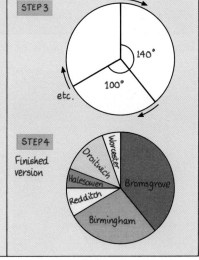

Figure 29.1 *Worked example: pie charts*

Shopped at	%	Angle
Bromsgrove	66	
Fairfield	6	
Worcester	6	
Kidderminster	17	
Others	5	

Figure 29.2 *Percentage of people from Bromsgrove shopping for garden and DIY goods*

FLOW CHARTS

Flow charts are used to show how things are linked. They can be used to describe a geographical system, like the water cycle (Figure 29.3), and to show how it works.

Flow charts can have:
- strong and weak links
- 1-way links
- 2-way links
- partial links
- barriers stopping links.

A flow chart is useful when you are trying to explain the results of a survey.

To design a flowchart:
- write out the subject of your flow chart in the centre of a piece of paper
- write down around the centre of the piece of paper, all the elements or factors which may be important to the subject
- link these elements together.

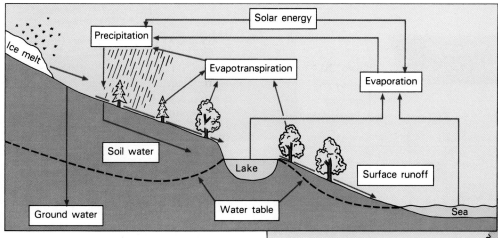

Figure 29.3
A flow chart:
the water cycle

FLOW MAPS

Flow maps plot the sizes of movements between places. They are used to show the links and the amount of linkage between places. They are useful for showing the results of transport surveys (Figure 29.4), for plotting population migrations and for showing exports and imports.

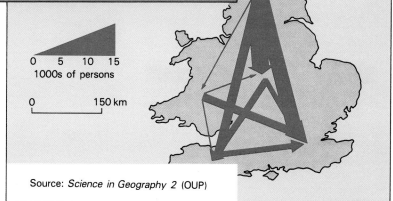

0 5 10 15
1000s of persons

0   150 km

Source: *Science in Geography 2* (OUP)

Figure 29.4 *A flow map: passenger journeys by train*

Things to do

1 **a** Draw a flow chart to describe the events that could happen at a crossroads as the traffic lights change to green.
  b Complete the flow chart by linking all the elements together.

2 **a** Draw a labelled flow chart to explain your usual journey to and from school.
  b Now add a list of possible events which might delay or prevent you from getting to school on time.
  c Complete your flow chart by linking these points.

3 Draw a large copy of the base map (Figure 29.5).

4 Look at the table of data in Figure 29.5.
  a What are the largest and smallest flows?
  b Work out and draw a key and scale for these movements.
  c Draw a flow map of the journeys to Oxford.

5 What does your flow map show about this area?

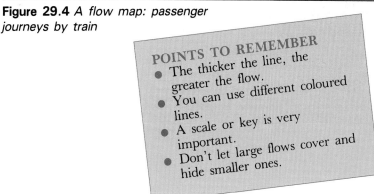

POINTS TO REMEMBER
● The thicker the line, the greater the flow.
● You can use different coloured lines.
● A scale or key is very important.
● Don't let large flows cover and hide smaller ones.

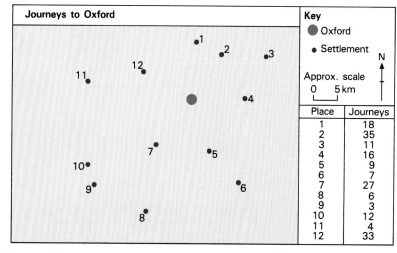

Place	Journeys
1	18
2	35
3	11
4	16
5	9
6	7
7	27
8	6
9	3
10	12
11	4
12	33

Figure 29.5 *Base map and data for journeys to Oxford*

30 Averages

Figure 30.1
Getting the most out of your data

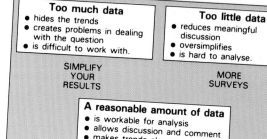

Too much data
- hides the trends
- creates problems in dealing with the question
- is difficult to work with.

SIMPLIFY YOUR RESULTS

Too little data
- reduces meaningful discussion
- oversimplifies
- is hard to analyse.

MORE SURVEYS

A reasonable amount of data
- is workable for analysis
- allows discussion and comment
- makes trends clearer.

STEP 1	STEP 1
Add up all the numbers you wish to average (A).	2 + 5 + 8 + 8 + 11 + 17 + 18 + 20 = 89
STEP 2	**STEP 2**
Count up how many figures you have added up (B).	8 numbers
STEP 3	**STEP 3**
Divide A by B.	89/8 = 11·1 = the mean Why has only one decimal place been used in the answer?

Figure 30.2 *Worked example: the mean*

An analysis of your results involves:
1 getting the main information out of your data (Figure 30.1)
2 making comparisons between the results you obtained
3 comparing your results with geographical principles
4 discussing what you have found out.

Averages help you to isolate and identify the main facts. They can be used to simplify data where there are too many numbers involved. Calculating averages allows patterns or trends to be identified from your raw data.

There are *three* ways of averaging data:
1 the mean
2 the median
3 the mode.

1 THE MEAN

The mean is the arithmetic average of the data (Figure 30.2). It is the

Things to do

1 Look at Figure 30.3, which shows six survey sites (A to F). Stone size was measured for 11 stones at each location.
  a Calculate the mean stone size for site A.
  b The mean stone sizes for the other sites are: B 58.2 cm; C 43.0 cm; D 53.3 cm; E 17.0 cm; and F 11.4 cm. How does the result for site A compare with the mean values for the other sites?
  c What effect does the tributary appear to have had on the mean stone size at site D?

2 Suggest two other cases (from fieldwork) where you would calculate the mean. For each example say why you would use the mean.

Stone diameter (D) Long axis ←—D—→ (cm)							Sketch map of river survey sites
Survey site Stone number	A	B	C	D	E	F	
1	86	66	42	74	14	7	
2	74	18	48	81	12	11	
3	71	94	41	40	14	8	
4	81	18	44	29	18	12	
5	70	62	40	27	19	9	
6	68	32	47	65	14	14	
7	82	81	41	49	21	19	
8	85	67	54	49	24	11	
9	70	80	35	38	16	9	
10	76	47	40	74	14	14	
11	79	75	41	60	21	11	

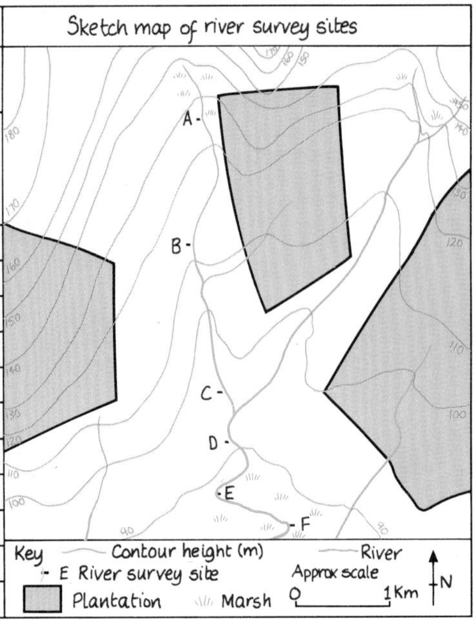

Key
Contour height (m) — River
- E River survey site
Plantation — Marsh
Approx scale 0 — 1 Km ↑N

Figure 30.3 *Stone size survey: sketch map and results*

2 THE MEDIAN

The median is the middle or central value of all the numbers (Figure 30.4). It has the same number of values above and below it. It therefore ignores values which are very small or large.

3 THE MODE

The mode is the number which occurs most frequently in the raw data. It is the simplest average to work out, but is the most limited.

Using the same figures as before, all the numbers occur once except 8, which is found twice. This is therefore the mode.

Study this set of figures:

4, 8, 8, 10, 10, 11, 12, 14

Here, 8 and 10 both occur more than any other number. There are therefore two modes (Figure 30.5).

POINTS TO REMEMBER
- You do not have to work out the mean, median and mode of your data. It is important that you choose the one which summarizes your information best. The mean is the best average to use in most cases as it is the most accurate.
- When analysing your results, you must comment on the actual data that was obtained by fieldwork, as well as any averages you may have calculated.

Things to do

1 Using the river data in Figure 30.3, work out the median and mode for survey site A.

2 Make a copy of the table of averages (Figure 30.6) and complete it by listing the results for the mean, median and mode at site A that you have calculated.

3 What do the results for site A show about mean stone size?

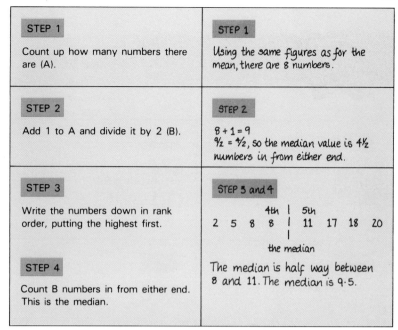

Figure 30.4 *Worked example: the median*

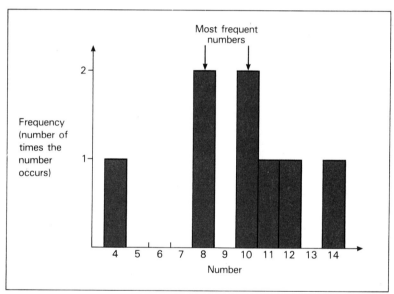

Figure 30.5 *A frequency graph showing two modes*

Site	Stone sizes (cm)		
	Mean	Median	Mode
A			
B	58·2	66·0	18·0
C	43·0	41·0	41·0
D	53·3	49·0	49·0 and 74·0
E	17·0	16·0	14·0
F	11·4	11·0	11·0

Figure 30.6 *Stone size survey: table of averages*

31 *Variation and spread*

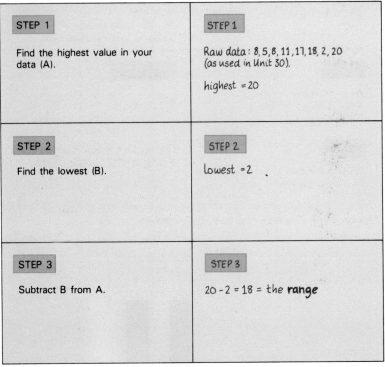

STEP 1	STEP 1
Find the highest value in your data (A).	Raw data: 8, 5, 8, 11, 17, 18, 2, 20 (as used in Unit 30). highest = 20
STEP 2	STEP 2
Find the lowest (B).	lowest = 2
STEP 3	STEP 3
Subtract B from A.	20 − 2 = 18 = the **range**

Figure 31.1 *Worked example: the range*

A spread shows the upper and lower limits of your data. Measures of spread are used to show you how varied your results are.

There are *three* measures of the spread of a set of figures:
1 the range
2 the inter-quartile range
3 the standard deviation.

1 THE RANGE

The range measures the complete spread of your data, from the highest to the lowest figure (Figure 31.1). It is the easiest to work out, but can be affected by extreme results.

The range is useful to:
● see if your data varies greatly
● show the complete spread of the results.

One or two extreme results will cause the range to be very large.

STEP 1	STEP 1
Calculate the median value (see Unit 30).	median = 9.5 (see Unit 30)
STEP 2	STEP 2
Divide the number of values + 1 by 4 (A).	8 values 8 + 1 = 9 9/4 = 2¼
STEP 3	STEP 3
Count A numbers in from each end. Subtract the lower number from the higher one.	Lowest value 2 5 8 8 11 12 17 18 20 Highest value 2¼ values in from lowest 2¼ values in from highest Lowest value 5·75 17·15 Highest value Inter-Quartile Range = 17·75 − 5·75 = 12·0

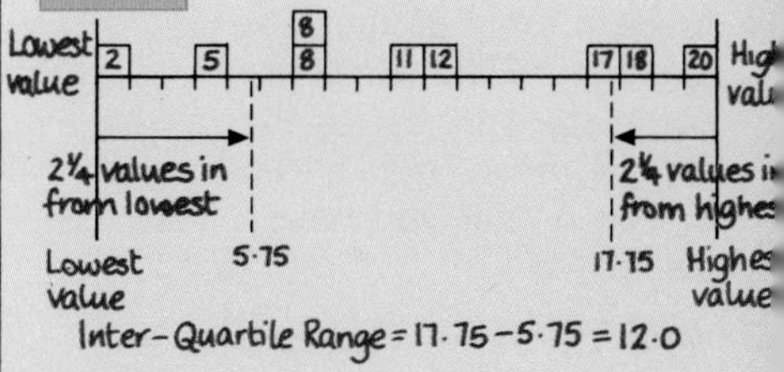

Figure 31.2 *Worked example: the inter-quartile range*

Things to do

1 Calculate the range of the data for each of the survey sites in Figure 30.3.

2 Which survey sites have a very large range of values?

3 Rivers tend to sort their deposits by size as they are moved downstream. Does your calculation back this up?

2 THE INTER-QUARTILE RANGE

The inter-quartile range is used with the median (Figure 31.2). It shows the amount of spread between the top quarter of the data and the bottom quarter. It does not include the top and bottom 25 per cent of the numbers in the calculation.

The inter-quartile range is useful as it ignores the extreme values. It is a reliable way to analyse the spread of your data.

3 THE STANDARD DEVIATION

The standard deviation measures by how much the figures differ from the mean (Figure 31.3). You can therefore calculate it when the mean is used.

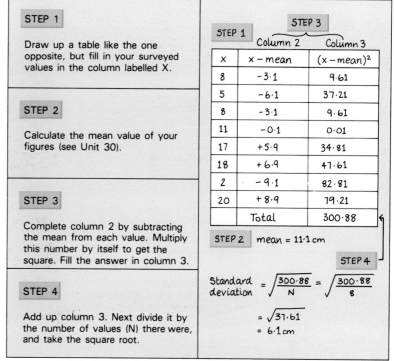

STEP 1

Draw up a table like the one opposite, but fill in your surveyed values in the column labelled X.

STEP 2

Calculate the mean value of your figures (see Unit 30).

STEP 3

Complete column 2 by subtracting the mean from each value. Multiply this number by itself to get the square. Fill the answer in column 3.

STEP 4

Add up column 3. Next divide it by the number of values (N) there were, and take the square root.

STEP 1	STEP 3 Column 2	Column 3
x	x − mean	(x − mean)²
8	−3.1	9.61
5	−6.1	37.21
8	−3.1	9.61
11	−0.1	0.01
17	+5.9	34.81
18	+6.9	47.61
2	−9.1	82.81
20	+8.9	79.21
	Total	300.88

STEP 2   mean = 11.1 cm

$$\text{Standard deviation} = \sqrt{\frac{300.88}{N}} = \sqrt{\frac{300.88}{8}}$$

$$= \sqrt{37.61}$$

$$= 6.1 \text{ cm}$$

Figure 31.3 *Worked example: the standard deviation*

POINTS TO REMEMBER
- Include units where they have been used.
- Your calculations are only as good as your least accurate survey. Do not use more than two decimal places.
- Standard deviation is the most complicated calculation, but it is the most reliable.

Things to do

1 a Calculate the inter-quartile range for site A in Figure 30.3 on page 62.

b The results for the other sites are: B = 48; C = 7; D = 36; E = 7; F = 5.
Compare these figures with the ranges.

c What do the results suggest?

2 Calculate the standard deviation of stone size at site A in Figure 30.3 on page 62.

3 The standard deviations for the other sites are: B 24.7 cm; C 4.8 cm; D 17.9 cm; E 3.7 cm; F 3.2 cm.

a Which survey sites had the greatest and the smallest deviation?

b What happens to the standard deviation of stone size as you move downstream (ignoring site D)?

c A sample of 11 stones was measured at each site. Do you think this was adequate?

WARNING!
- Many of these calculations are not essential to your coursework. They are only useful if you understand what the results mean. It is much better to carry out a simple analysis which allows you to discuss your findings clearly than to introduce complicated calculations that confuse you.
- Select the methods of simplifying your data carefully and say why you decided to analyse your data that way.
- Always show all your calculations.

32 Rank-size and the Lorenz curve

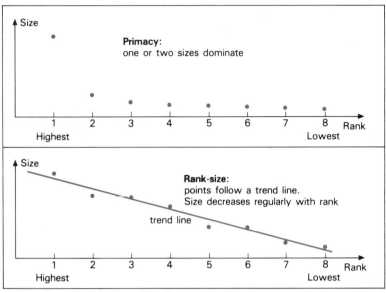

Figure 32.1 *Primacy and rank-size graphs*

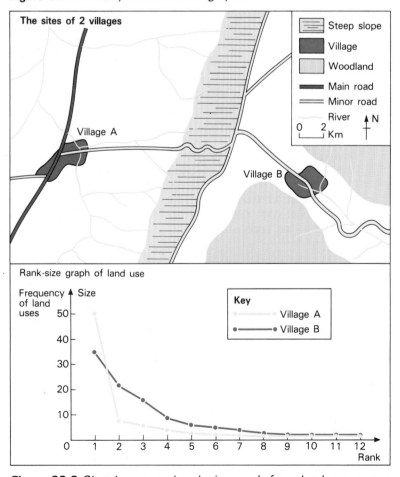

Figure 32.3 *Sketch map and rank-size graph for a land use survey*

RANK-SIZE

You will often need to compare several sets of data. One way of doing this is to draw a rank-size graph.

Ranking the data means putting it in order, with the largest value first and finishing with the smallest. A rank-size graph therefore plots the size of the value against its rank (Figure 32.1).

Rank-size can be used to study hierarchies, for example settlements can be ordered and grouped into those which have similar sizes (Figure 32.2).

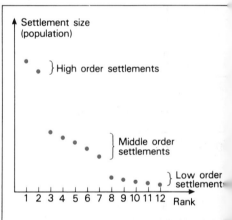

Figure 32.2 *Rank-size graph of a settlement hierarchy*

Things to do

1 Study the sketch map and graph in Figure 32.3.
   a How do villages A and B differ in their location?
   b How are villages A and B different in their largest land uses?
   c If A was a commuter village, what do you think would be its main land use?

2 a Draw a rank-size graph for the data given in Figure 32.4.
   b What evidence does your graph and Figure 32.3 give you about the ways land is used in these villages?

THE LORENZ CURVE

The Lorenz curve is another way of comparing sets of information on a graph. It is a cumulative frequency graph. The data is accumulated as shown in Figure 32.5.

The Lorenz curve can be used to compare:

- regions, areas or different times (use percentage values if the data sets don't add up to the same number)
- types of activity, like employment or farming
- how evenly spread or concentrated the data is (Figure 32.5).

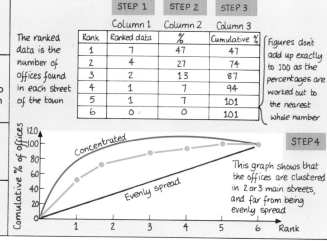

	Rank	1	2	3	4	5	6	7	8	9
Village A	% area	61	10	9	5	5	3	3	2	2
	Use	Housing	Recreation	Farming	Shops	Village activities	Transport	Offices	Waste/open space	Others
Village B	Rank	1	2	3	4	5	6	7	8	
	% area	39	20	15	10	10	3	2	1	
	Use	Housing	Farming	Waste/Open space	Village activities	Transport	Shops	Recreation	Others	

Figure 32.4 Land use areas in villages A and B

STEP 1

Draw up a table like the one shown opposite. Rank (place in order) the figures and fill in column 1 with the ranked raw data.

STEP 2

Work out the percentage value for each piece of raw data. To do this, divide the data value by the total and multiply by 100. Fill in column 2. Repeat for each piece of data.

STEP 3

Cumulate the numbers (add each number in turn to the total of the numbers above it) and complete column 3 of the table.

STEP 4

Plot the cumulated figures against their rank.

The ranked data is the number of offices found in each street of the town

| STEP 1 | STEP 2 | STEP 3 |
Rank	Ranked data	%	Cumulative %
1	7	47	47
2	4	27	74
3	2	13	87
4	1	7	94
5	1	7	101
6	0	0	101

Figures don't add up exactly to 100 as the percentages are worked out to the nearest whole number

STEP 4: This graph shows that the offices are clustered in 2 or 3 main streets, and far from being evenly spread

Figure 32.5 Worked example: the Lorenz curve

Things to do

1. Make a copy of the table of survey results in Figure 32.6.

2. Put the survey sites in rank order by height, lowest first.

3. Work out the total number of trees and bushes.

4. Calculate the percentage number of trees and bushes found at each site.

5. Work out the cumulative percentage for each.

6. Construct a Lorenz curve for the survey results in Figure 32.6.

7. How could you plot the data for percentage grass cover on the same graph?

8. Describe the changes in vegetation that occur along the profile in Figure 32.6.

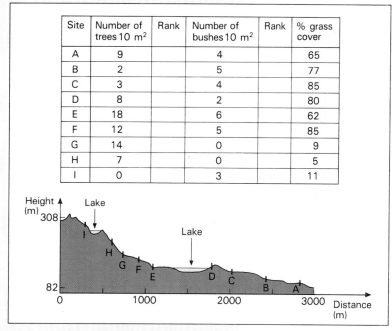

Site	Number of trees 10 m²	Rank	Number of bushes 10 m²	Rank	% grass cover
A	9		4		65
B	2		5		77
C	3		4		85
D	8		2		80
E	18		6		62
F	12		5		85
G	14		0		9
H	7		0		5
I	0		3		11

Figure 32.6 Vegetation survey results and profile

33 *Using models*

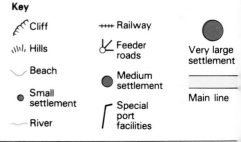

Figure 33.1

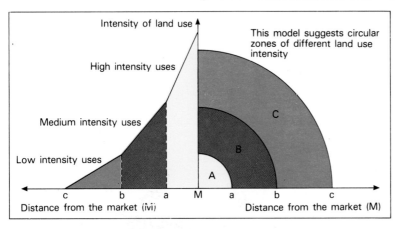

Intensity of land use

This model suggests circular zones of different land use intensity

High intensity uses

Medium intensity uses

Low intensity uses

C

B

A

c   b   a   M   a   b   c

Distance from the market (M)   Distance from the market (M)

Models simplify reality (Figure 33.1). They are used to show *what* could happen and *how* things might happen (the processes). They also show what is expected to happen in a simplified situation.

Figure 33.2 shows a model of agricultural patterns. This model looks at how much the land is used for agriculture, comparing it with how close the land is to the local market. The model suggests that the most used (or intensive) farming land will be found nearest the market.

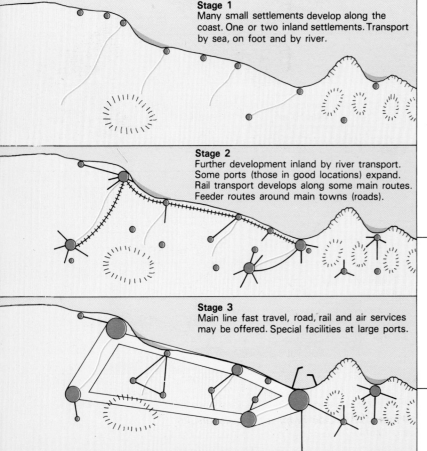

Stage 1
Many small settlements develop along the coast. One or two inland settlements. Transport by sea, on foot and by river.

Stage 2
Further development inland by river transport. Some ports (those in good locations) expand. Rail transport develops along some main routes. Feeder routes around main towns (roads).

Stage 3
Main line fast travel, road, rail and air services may be offered. Special facilities at large ports.

Figure 33.3 shows a model for looking at the development of transport routes. It shows the earliest routes developing around ports. As the transport network develops, the largest cities will attract the biggest routes.

Successful enquiries can compare fieldwork surveys with a model situation. To do this, you will need to:
● understand the model
● select carefully what you will survey
● decide how to compare your results with the model.

Key

 ⌒ Cliff   +++ Railway

 �al۱ا Hills   ⅄ Feeder roads   ● Very large settlement

 ⌒ Beach

 ● Small settlement   ● Medium settlement   ── Main line

 ⌒ River   ⌐ Special port facilities

Figure 33.3 *Model of transport development*

HOW TO USE THE MODEL

1 Understand the basic principles of the model (Figure 33.4).
2 You may need to alter the model (Figure 33.5) in order to fit it to your local situation or enquiry.
3 Carry out your survey and draw up your results (Figure 33.6).
4 Plot your surveyed results (Figure 33.7).

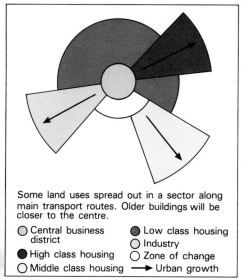

Some land uses spread out in a sector along main transport routes. Older buildings will be closer to the centre.
○ Central business district
● High class housing
○ Middle class housing
● Low class housing
○ Industry
○ Zone of change
→ Urban growth

Figure 33.4 *Sector model of urban land use: basic principles*

Things to do

1 What is the most important factor in the location of land uses in Figure 33.4?

2 What changes were made to the model in Figure 33.5?

3 a Which parts of Bristol (Figure 33.7) fit the model?
  b Which ones differ?
  c What might have caused these differences?
  d How might you change the model to include recent inner city and suburban developments?

4 Choose either the agricultural or transport model in this Unit.
  a Write a list of the basic ideas behind the model.
  b Alter the model to fit your local area.
  c What data will you need to collect?
  d How could you present your findings?

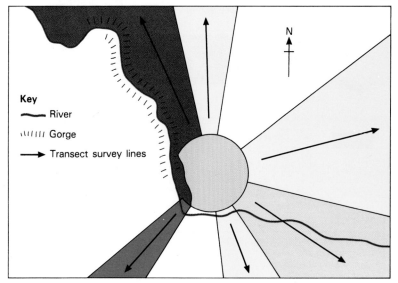

Figure 33.5 *Some predicted urban transects in Bristol*

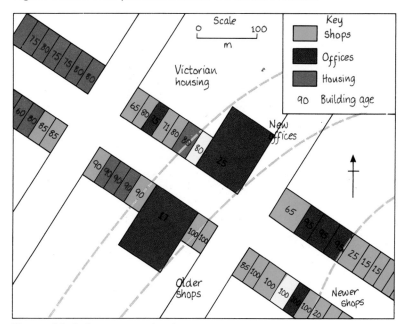

Figure 33.6 *Survey results for urban land use*

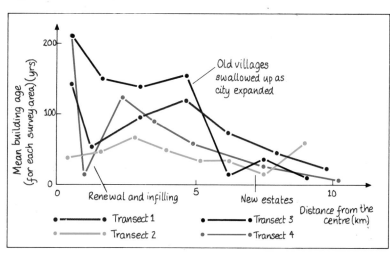

Figure 33.7 *Line graph of survey results*

34 Connections, links and nodes

STEP 1

Count up the number of nodes (N) and links (L).

STEP 2

Divide the number of links (L) by the number of nodes (N) to work out the number of links per node in the network.
This is the **actual connectivity** of the network.

STEP 3

Calculate the number of links needed for each node to be connected to all the others (S). Do this by:

$$S = \frac{N \times (N-1)}{2}$$ (N = number of nodes)

STEP 4

Calculate the **maximum connectivity** of the network and then compare the actual connectivity with the maximum.

$$\text{maximum connectivity} = \frac{S}{N}$$

• Node
— Link

STEP 1

nodes = 12 links = 16

STEP 2

$$\frac{L}{N} = \frac{16}{12} = 1.33$$

STEP 3

$$S = \frac{12 \times 11}{2} = 66$$

STEP 4

$$\frac{S}{N} = \frac{66}{12} = 5.5$$

$$\frac{actual}{maximum} = \frac{1.33}{5.5} = 0.24$$

The island is about one-quarter connected.

Figure 34.1 *Worked example: connectivity*

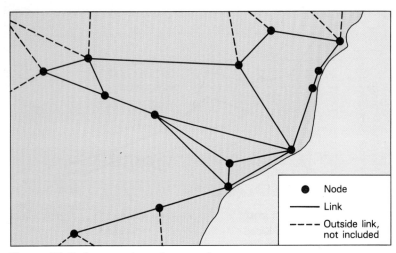

Figure 34.2 *A coastal road network*

• Node
— Link
- - - Outside link, not included

A network is a series of communication lines (or **links**) which join up places (or **nodes**) on a map, as shown in Figure 34.1.

Transport networks can be analysed in three ways:
1 connectivity
2 detour
3 centrality.

1 CONNECTIVITY

This is how well the points on the network are connected to one another. You can measure the connectivity of the network by counting how many links there are with each node (Figure 34.1).

2 DETOUR

The amount of detour compares the actual transport routes with the most direct way of going from one place to another (Figure 34.3).

POINTS TO REMEMBER
- It is impossible to have a detour of less than 100.
- The most direct route has a detour closest to 100.
- The bigger the answer the greater the detour.

3 CENTRALITY

This measures how central places are in a network. The most important places tend to be the most central so that they are easily accessible from other places.

Things to do

1 a Calculate the connectivity of the network in Figure 34.2.
  b Now calculate the maximum connectivity.
  c Compare the results.

2 Explain why it is unlikely that any one node would be directly connected to all the others.

3 Why is the island network calculation more accurate than the coastal one?

STEP 1
Measure the straight-line distance (A) between 2 nodes.

STEP 2
Measure the distance along the chosen route between the 2 nodes (B).

STEP 3
Calculate $\frac{B}{A} \times 100$.
Subtract this figure from 100. This is the percentage detour.

STEP 1

A = 14cm

STEP 2

B = 21cm

STEP 3 $\frac{B}{A} \times 100 = \frac{21}{14} \times 100 = 150$ This route has a 50% detour.

Figure 34.3 *Worked example: detour*

A simple measure of centrality is to count the number of links that have to be crossed to reach the furthest place on the network. The smaller the number of links, the more central the place is. For a large network, it is best to draw up a matrix of all the points and count the number of links that you would cross to reach each node by the shortest possible route. Figure 34.5 shows a matrix for the towns in Figure 34.4.

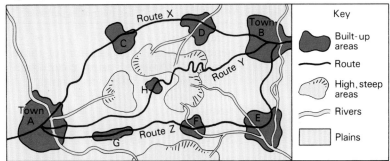

Figure 34.4 *Detours between two towns*

Things to do

1 Compare the detour of the three routes X, Y and Z between the two towns A and B shown in Figure 34.4.

2 What do you think might slow down traffic on route X?

3 What factors other than distance do you think need to be considered to give a better measure of detour?

4 a Number the places on the island network (Figure 34.1).
  b Draw a matrix for these places.
  c Count the number of links you have to cross to go from each node to every other one.
  d For each node, which is the furthest place? How many links must be crossed to reach it?
  e Which node is the most centrally placed?

etwork analysis has a number of roblems:
  The effect of boundaries and the edge of the survey area is not accounted for. You must select carefully the limits of your survey area.

	B & A, 2 nodes by the shortest route				Centrality of each town				
From To	A	B	C	D	E	F	G	H	Total
A	—	2	1	2	3	2	1	1	12
B	2	—	2	1	1	2	3	1	12
C	1	2	—	1	3	3	2	2	14
D	2	1	1	—	2	3	3	2	14
E	3	1	3	2	—	1	2	2	14
F	2	2	3	3	1	—	1	3	15
G	1	3	2	3	2	1	—	2	14
H	1	1	2	2	2	3	2	—	13

A and B are most central as they have the lowest value.

F is least central as it has the highest total.

- The time taken to travel may be more important than distance or the number of links crossed.
- The frequency of service and the cost are often important.
- You should also consider the comfort, ease of use and convenience of a route.
- No account is taken of the size or importance of the links in the analysis.

Figure 34.5 *Centrality matrix*

35 Correlation

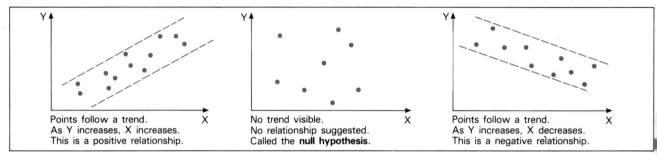

Points follow a trend. X As Y increases, X increases. This is a positive relationship.	No trend visible. X No relationship suggested. Called the **null hypothesis**.	Points follow a trend. X As Y increases, X decreases. This is a negative relationship.

Figure 35.1
Scattergraphs and trends

Scattergraphs (Figure 35.1) show general trends. The amount of these trends is calculated using correlation. If all the points follow the trend, there is said to be a perfect relationship.

SIMPLE CORRELATION

A simple comparison can be carried out by calculating Spearman's rank correlation (Figure 35.2). This calculation shows the general trends by using ranked or ordered data.

Figure 35.2 *Worked example: Spearman's rank correlation*

The answer you obtain must lie between $+1.0$ and -1.0. If you get a smaller or larger total, then you have made a mistake in your calculation.

WHAT THE RESULT MEANS

$$+1.0 \longleftarrow 0 \longrightarrow -1.0$$

a perfect positive relationship   no relationship   a perfect negative relationship

The closer to $+1.0$, the stronger the positive relationship between Y and X. The closer to -1.0, the stronger the negative relationship.
The nearer to 0, the weaker the link between X and Y.

STEP 1

Draw up a table as shown here. Fill in the matching values of the 2 surveyed quantities X (% humidity) and Y (height, in metres) into columns 1 and 2.

STEP 2

Rank (put in order) the values of X and then those of Y and fill in columns 3 and 4.

STEP 3

Complete column 5 by calculating the difference (D) between the ranks of X and Y.

STEP 4

Square each number in column 5 and fill in column 6 (D²). Add up column 6.

STEP 5

Calculate Spearman's rank correlation by completing the formula:

$$\text{rank correlation} = 1 - \frac{6 \times \text{total of column 6}}{n(n^2 - n)}$$

where n is the number of points on your graph.

STEP 6

What does the result mean?

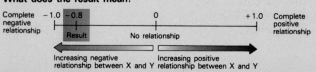

Complete negative relationship -1.0 -0.8 0 $+1.0$ Complete positive relationship

Result   No relationship

Increasing negative relationship between X and Y   Increasing positive relationship between X and Y

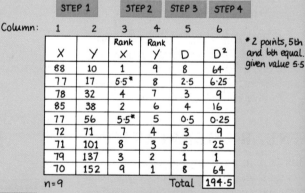

STEP 1		STEP 2	STEP 3	STEP 4	
Column: 1	2	3	4	5	6
X	Y	Rank X	Rank Y	D	D²
88	10	1	9	8	64
77	17	5.5*	8	2.5	6.25
78	32	4	7	3	9
85	38	2	6	4	16
77	56	5.5*	5	0.5	0.25
72	71	7	4	3	9
71	101	8	3	5	25
79	137	3	2	1	1
70	152	9	1	8	64

n=9   Total 194.5

* 2 points, 5th and 6th equal. given value 5.5

STEP 5

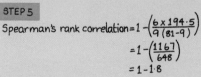

$$\text{Spearman's rank correlation} = 1 - \left(\frac{6 \times 194.5}{9(81-9)}\right)$$

$$= 1 - \left(\frac{1167}{648}\right)$$

$$= 1 - 1.8$$

$$= -0.8$$

This is quite a high negative relationship.

STEP 6

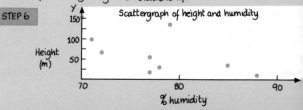

Scattergraph of height and humidity

Draw up the table and fill in the values of X (mean river speed, in cm/s) and Y (mean suspended sediment weight, in g) in columns 1 and 2.

STEP 2

For each value of X, square it and put the answer in column 3. Do the same for Y and put the result in column 4.

STEP 3

Multiply each value of X by its corresponding value of Y. Put the answer in column 5.

STEP 4

Add up all the columns, n = the number of points.

STEP 5

Complete the calculation using the formula:
n = number of points = 12

Complete the calculation using the formula :

$$\text{correlation} = \frac{(n \times \text{column 15}) - (\text{column 1} \times \text{column 2})}{\sqrt{\left[(n \times \text{Total 3}) - (\text{Total 1})^2\right] \times \left[(n \times \text{Total 4}) - (\text{Total 2})^2\right]}}$$

$$C = \frac{(12 \times 241.22) - (576 \times 5.25)}{\sqrt{\left[(12 \times 28 + 14) - (576)^2\right] \times \left[(12 \times 2.67) - (5.25)^2\right]}} = \frac{2894.64 - 3024}{\sqrt{(340968 - 331776) \times (32.04 - 27.6)}}$$

$$C = \frac{-129.36}{\sqrt{9192 \times 4.44}} = \frac{-129.36}{\sqrt{41180}} = \frac{-129.36}{\sqrt{203}} = -0.62$$

The linear correlation coefficient, C = **−0.62**.

	Column 1	Column 2	Column 3	Column 4	Column 5
	Mean river speed Cm/S (X)	Mean suspended sediment weight (g) (Y)	X^2	Y^2	XY
	38.25	0.40	1463.06	0.16	15.30
	41.0	0.54	1681	0.29	22.14
	46.0	0.40	2116	0.16	18.40
	47.25	0.82	2232.56	0.67	38.75
	49.25	0.46	2425.56	0.21	22.66
	35.00	0.66	1225	0.44	23.10
	53.00	0.38	2809	0.14	20.14
	53.75	0.26	2889.06	0.07	13.98
	54.00	0.25	2916	0.06	13.50
	40.00	0.58	1600	0.34	23.20
	63.50	0.30	4032.25	0.09	19.05
	55.00	0.20	3025	0.04	11.00
STEP 4 Total	576.00	5.25	28 414	2.67	241.22
	Total 1	Total 2	Total 3	Total 4	Total 5

Figure 35.3 *Worked example: linear correlation*

Things to do

1 From the worked example (Figure 35.2), was there a relationship between percentage humidity and height?

2 a From the graph in Figure 35.2, which results did not follow the general trend?
   b Suggest what may have been responsible for these results.
   c What other surveyed information might have helped you understand the results?

LINEAR CORRELATION

This is a more complex calculation. It calculates whether there is a linear or straight-line relationship between the two variables X and Y and not if there is a general trend (Figure 35.3). It uses the raw data and does not involve ranking. Again, the answer must lie between +1.0 and −1.0.

WARNING! This can be a very long calculation. It may be quicker to use a programmable calculator or a computer program. The result is important and its meaning, not how it was calculated.

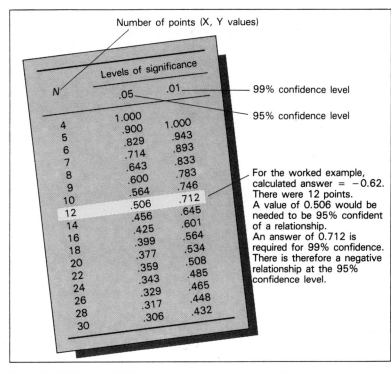

Number of points (X, Y values)

Levels of significance

N	.05	.01
4	1.000	
5	.900	1.000
6	.829	.943
7	.714	.893
8	.643	.833
9	.600	.783
10	.564	.746
12	.506	.712
14	.456	.645
16	.425	.601
18	.399	.564
20	.377	.534
22	.359	.508
24	.343	.485
26	.329	.465
28	.317	.448
30	.306	.432

99% confidence level

95% confidence level

For the worked example, calculated answer = −0.62. There were 12 points. A value of 0.506 would be needed to be 95% confident of a relationship. An answer of 0.712 is required for 99% confidence. There is therefore a negative relationship at the 95% confidence level.

SIGNIFICANCE

You can show the amount of correlation by using significance tables (Figure 35.4). These give a measure of how likely it is that the results occurred by chance. The greater the correlation, the less likely it is that chance factors were important.

You should always comment on the level of significance of your correlation calculation.

Figure 35.4 *Significance table: critical values for Spearman's rank correlation*

36 *Nearest neighbour*

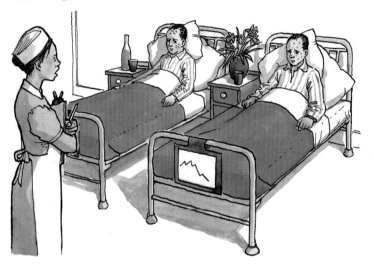

Points grouped or spread on a map show important trends. These trends need to be analysed (Figure 36.1). Nearest neighbour analysis calculates the amount of clustering (or grouping) and how spread out (dispersed) a set of points is (Figure 36.2).

The nearest neighbour statistic, NN, must *always* have a value between 0 and 2.15. If it does not, then you have probably made an error in your calculation.

Figure 36.1 *Spot the difference!*

STEP 1

Measure the distance from each point to its nearest neighbour and write it down.

STEP 2

Add up all the distances you have measured (D). Check that you have the same number of distances as points on the map. Calculate the average distance.

STEP 3

Work out the surveyed map area (A) and count the number of points (N).

STEP 4

Calculate the nearest neighbour statistic (NN) using the formula:

$$NN = 2 \times D \sqrt{\frac{N}{A}}$$

Point pattern

STEP 1

Point	Nearest neighbour	Distance (cm)
1	2	1·0
2	3	0·5
3	2	0·5
4	5	0·75
5	4	0·75
6	7	0·5
7	6	0·5
8	3	1·6
Total		6·1

STEP 2

$D = 6·1$ cm

Average $= \frac{6·1}{8} = 0·76$

STEP 3

$A = 4$ cm $\times 6$ cm $= 24$ cm^2

$N = 8$ points

STEP 4

$NN = 2 \times 0·76 \sqrt{\frac{8}{24}}$

$NN = 0·88$

Figure 36.2 *Worked example: nearest neighbour analysis*

SOME COMMON ERRORS

- Distance and area must be measured in the same units, e.g. km.
- Calculate N/A before taking the square root.
- Check that you have measured the same number of distances as points.

WHAT DOES THE RESULT MEAN?
(Figure 36.3)

If NN = 0 then the points are completely clustered.
A result of 2.15 means the points are completely spread out.
The closer to 0, the more clustered the points are. The nearer to 2.15, the more spread the points are.

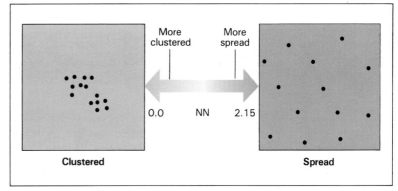

Figure 36.3 *Clustered and spread point patterns*

PROBLEMS

1 This analysis only measures the distance to one nearest neighbour. In Figure 36.4, the points are spread out but in small clusters. Nearest neighbour analysis would give a clustered result.
2 The survey area boundaries may hide nearest neighbours which are just off the map, causing the calculation to be inaccurate. Select your survey area with this in mind.
3 The distances are normally measured in straight lines. Distance by road, the cost or travel time may be better measures.
4 The points are all assumed to be the same size. No differences in importance are included.

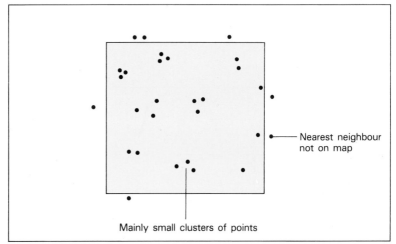

Figure 36.4 *Problems of analysis*

USING NEAREST NEIGHBOUR

Nearest neighbour can be used:
- for all types of point patterns
- to compare different places or patterns
- to compare with a completely spread or clustered pattern.

Things to do

1 a Trace or copy the boundaries of Figure 36.5.
  b Mark each farm on your map with a point.
  c What pattern does your set of points appear to suggest?

2 Calculate the nearest neighbour statistic for the point pattern.

3 What does your result suggest about the location of farms?

4 What factors might explain your answer?

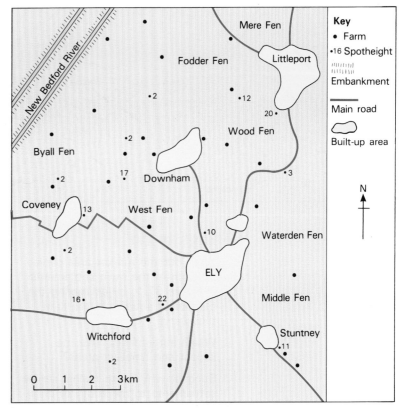

Figure 36.5 *Sketch map of Ely and its surrounding area*

Market areas and the Gravity Model

If you carry out a survey of where people come from to use the facilities in a town, you can then draw a map to show the area influenced by the settlement (Figure 37.1). This is called the market area.

MARKET AREAS

Large settlements draw people in from greater distances than smaller ones.

If you map your survey data on squared paper and draw a boundary around the area people come from, you can work out the market area by counting the number of squares. Settlement size, number of functions and market area are then easily compared (Figure 37.2).

Figure 37.1 *Market areas in NE England*

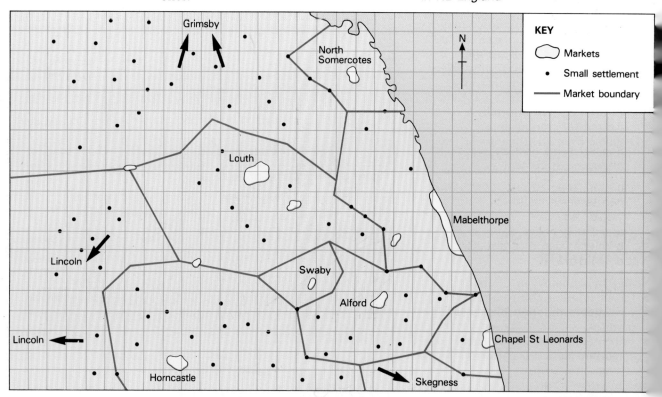

Things to do

1   Work out the market area served by each of the main settlements in Figure 37.1, by estimating the number of squares in the area they serve.

2   Which settlements have the largest and smallest areas?

3   Suggest why Louth mainly serves settlements to the south of it.

4   What relationships are shown in Figure 37.2 between settlement size, number of functions and the areas served by these settlements?

5   Models suggest a hierarchy or ordering of settlements (Figure 37.3). Similar settlements are evenly spaced. Larger centres are further apart than smaller ones. Why should this be so?

6   Why are there many more smaller settlements than larger ones in Figure 37.3?

THE GRAVITY MODEL

The Gravity Model predicts the number of journeys that you expect to be made between places. It is based on the principle that the bigger the settlement, the greater its pulling power.

The distance between two places also affects how many people will travel between them. Settlements close to one another will tend to have more journeys made between them than those which are far apart (Figure 37.4). As the distance increases, the pulling power of the settlement quickly decays (Figure 37.5).

The number of journeys (T) between two settlements A and B is predicted by the Gravity Model. It is calculated using the formula:

$$T = \frac{\text{size of settlement A} \times \text{size of settlement B}}{(\text{distance from A to B})^2}$$

Things to do

1 Suggest some possible ways of measuring settlement size.

2 If there were several roads linking two settlements, which distance would you use:
  a the straight-line distance
  b the shortest road distance
  c the average distance?
  Explain the reasons for your choice.

3 Suggest why the following towns will have more journeys to them than expected, and when the movements will be greatest:
  a seaside town
  b market town
  c boom town.

4 a Measure the diameter of each settlement in Figure 37.4.
  b Measure the distances the settlements are apart.
  c Calculate T using the Gravity Model for the settlements.
  d What factors might reduce the number of people moving between the two largest settlements in Figure 37.4?

5 a Explain how you would carry out a survey to test the Gravity Model in your area.

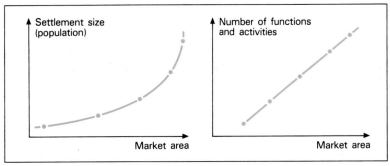

Figure 37.2 *Market area, settlement size and number of functions: predicted relationships*

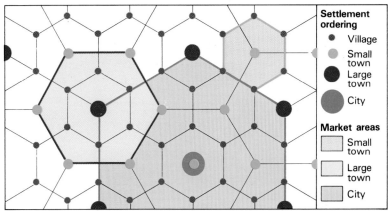

Figure 37.3 *Settlement hierarchy and market areas: a model case*

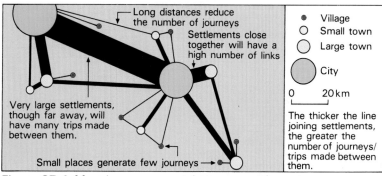

Figure 37.4 *Mapping movement between settlements*

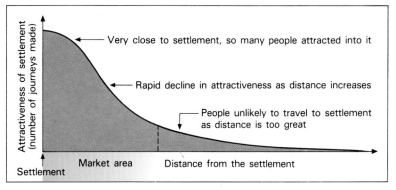

b Write out the hypothesis you would test.
c What data would you need to collect and how would you get it?

Figure 37.5 *The attractiveness of settlements*

Presenting your work

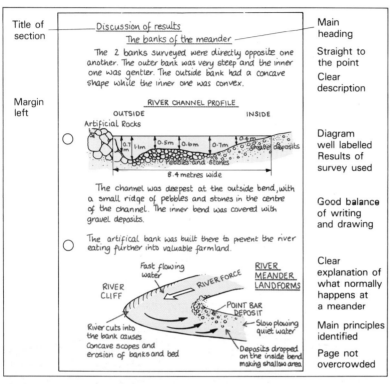

Title of section	Main heading
	Straight to the point
	Clear description
Margin left	
	Diagram well labelled Results of survey used
	Good balance of writing and drawing
	Clear explanation of what normally happens at a meander
	Main principles identified
	Page not overcrowded

Figure 38.1 *An attractive layout: get the right balance*

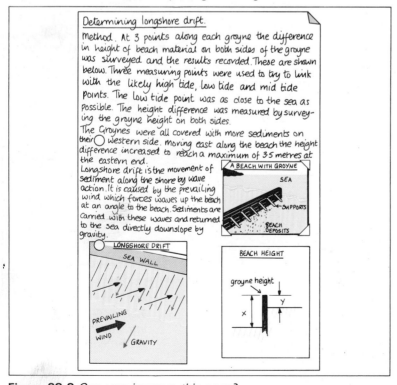

Figure 38.3 *Can you improve this page?*

The way you present your coursework is very important (Figure 38.1).

PAGE LAYOUT

First impressions count. Present your work carefully and neatly. A well presented study naturally creates a good impression. It can help you

Figure 38.2 *Make sure your work is easy to read!*

Things to do

Look carefully at Figure 38.3.

1 What would you add to Figure 38.3 to make it clearer and easie to follow?

2 How would you organize the pag to give it a better balance?

3 How could you use the illustrations better?

4 Copy out the two checklists (Figures 38.4 and 38.5). When

relate illustrations to text. Any report needs to be clear to read (Figure 38.2), and dividing up the work can help you keep your ideas organized.

DIAGRAMS AND GRAPHS

Draw diagrams on plain paper if possible. Use capital letters or print the letters carefully to make diagrams clear. Graphs should be drawn on graph paper. Do not include graphs or diagrams if you then ignore them in your write-up (Figure 38.3).

MAPS

Maps should be drawn on plain paper. It is a good idea to make a rough sketch first, then draw your map neatly (Figure 38.6).

Write information on maps in ink. Either use capital letters or print the letters carefully. Shade in different areas and include a key. Make sure you discuss each illustration in your written work.

PHOTOGRAPHS

If you want to use photographs, make sure you take them early as they must be developed before you hand in your coursework.

- Attach photographs firmly on to your work.
- Label and title each one.
- Use the photographs to help you explain your results and to describe what you found out. You can overlay your illustrations with clear film or tracing paper to label them.

you write up your coursework, use these checklists to help you draw each map, graph or illustration.

5 a Study Figure 38.6. Write out what needs to be done to improve this sketch map.
 b Which labels are not adequate? What needs to be added to them?
 c How could the title be improved?

POINTS TO REMEMBER
- You should try to give your work an attractive layout.
- Underline titles and headings carefully with a ruler.
- Underline clearly your main findings and the most important points you want to make.
- Avoid some of your work being hidden beneath the binding by leaving a wide enough margin on the left hand side of each page.
- Do not put too much information on one page. Spread it out, and leave enough space.
- Do not write your work in red or green ink.
- You must record and state *facts* clearly and concisely.
- Make sure your work is easy to read.
- Work done on a typewriter or wordprocessor is acceptable, if it is typed by you.

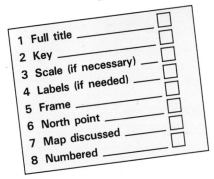

Figure 38.4 Checklist: maps

Figure 38.5 Checklist: illustrations

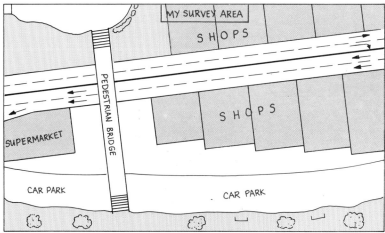

Figure 38.6 Sketch map of a survey area

39 *The key sections*

Figure 39.1 *You will need to do some detective work to find patterns and answers!*

POINTS TO REMEMBER
- Start each of these sections on a new page.
- The titles indicate what you will be discussing in each section.
- Remember that teachers are allowed to give you guidance on most sections of your enquiry. If you need help, ask for it.
- Balance your written work between the sections. Don't over-stress one part, while doing very little on another.
- Make your write-up easy to follow for the teacher who marks your work.
- Try to lead from one section into another by saying what comes next.
- You should try to have a clear line of argument.

Imagine you are exploring a new area and that you want to investigate what is happening there. You have a number of interests, so you decide to keep detailed and accurate records of what you see. You then decide to sift through your records to assess what has been happening.

This is just like a fieldwork enquiry. When you write up your enquiry you will be exploring what happened and trying to detect patterns and answers (Figure 39.1). You will end up by drawing together the main points to form conclusions.

PROJECT DESIGN

A fieldwork enquiry needs to have the following sections:
- introduction
- aim (which can include questions to answer) and hypothesis
- study method
- results
- data processing and analysis
- discussion
- conclusions.

INTRODUCTION

This should include basic facts about:
- the study area. Include a location map (Figure 39.2)
- the subject you are studying.

AIMS OR OBJECTIVES

Your aims need to be clearly defined. Write down what you are trying to find out. The more specific you are the more likely you are to achieve your aims.

Answer the following questions for your enquiry:
- What are you trying to do?
- What information do you need to collect?
- Is there a problem you are trying to study?

HYPOTHESIS

What results will you expect to find? Will there be any relationships or trends? What factors will be most important?

STUDY METHOD

Explain how you obtained your results. This is how the information *was* collected. You must therefore write it in the *past tense*, in the order that you did the survey.

Any decisions that you made must be explained here, such as the type of sample you took, the number of surveys you did and how you collected the data. Some syllabuses ask you to state exactly what part *you* played in data collection, if you worked in a group.

In your description include:
- a sketch map and diagram of how and why survey sites were selected and where they were
- a drawing of the equipment you used
- how the equipment was used to obtain the data (Figure 39.3)
- any questionnaires that you designed
- a comment about the reasons for each of the questions and the survey design, for example its length.

RESULTS

Present your results neatly and clearly.
Include:
  a **visual** presentation in the form of graphs, diagrams, illustrations, maps, etc.
  a **numerical** presentation in the form of tables.

Most syllabuses require a **variety** of presentations. Make sure, however, that the ways you choose are **meaningful** and **appropriate** to your data and to your particular study.

ANALYSIS

Your analysis needs to simplify and present the main facts in a clear, concise way. Describe carefully any trends or patterns shown by your illustrations. Comment on the accuracy of any measurements and surveys you did. Concentrate on patterns and **trends**.

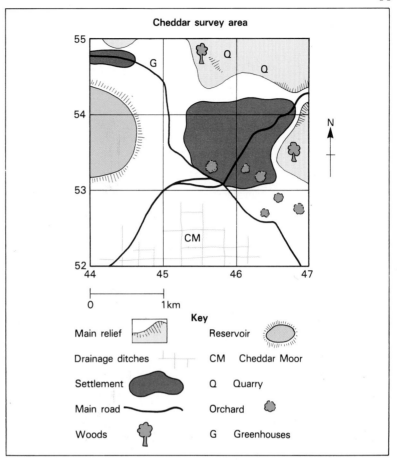

Figure 39.2 *Locating your survey*

Figure 39.3 *How was your equipment used?*

Things to do

1 Write a list of the questions you need to answer for each of the sections of your write-up.

2 Now design a checklist for your write-up.

40 *Completing your enquiry*

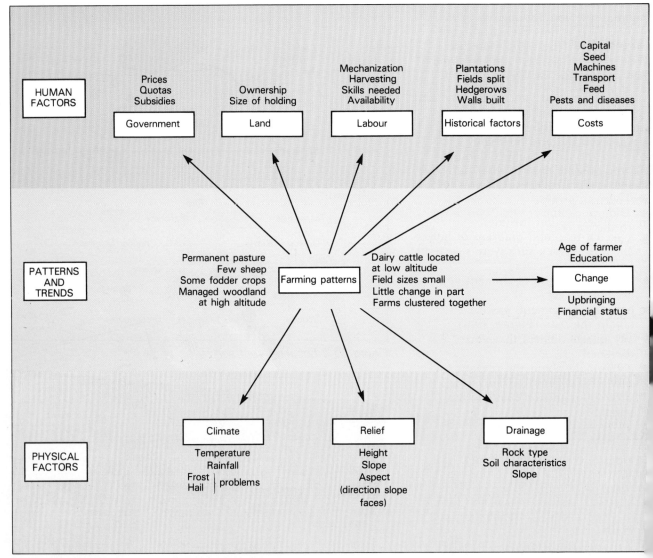

Figure 40.1 *Flow chart of processes and factors*

DISCUSSION

In this section of your write-up, describe what you found out. Include a discussion of any patterns and trends. Try to suggest reasons which help to explain your results and the patterns and trends you have noticed.

Two questions you will need to ask are:
1 What do you think could have caused the results you obtained?
2 Were they what you expected?

Write a summary of the investigation here. It should include a list of:

● **Processes** that were happening when you carried out your survey. Processes explain how things happen.
● **Factors** which caused your results to turn out the way they did. Factors explain why you got your results.

Design a flow chart of processes and factors as you do your enquiry (Figure 40.1). Consider both human and physical factors. Remember that your survey may have been influenced by things outside the immediate area of your study.

Include in your discussion any:
- limitations your study had
- problems you had with the survey
- difficulties you found in explaining your results.

CONCLUSIONS

(Figure 40.2)
Write a conclusion for each section of your write-up. The final conclusion of your study must answer the original questions or study aims. Read your aims through before writing this section. A list of your findings is essential.

Answer these questions in your conclusion:
- Have you achieved your aims?
- Did you find out what you set out to discover?
- What further questions does your study pose?

Figure 40.2 *At last! summing up*

SPECIAL PAGES

Some special pages you may need include:
- cover
- title-page (Figure 40.3a)
- contents page (Figure 40.3b)
- appendix
- bibliography.

A stiff cover will help to keep your write-up neat. Begin each enquiry with its own title-page. Use a contents page to list what you have written.

Use an appendix to put in all your completed survey sheets. The raw data should be included, even if it is not very neat. Place any special references or secondary sources in an appendix. Copies of letters and survey sheets should be in an appendix, as well as an acknowledgement of any help you have been given.

Avoid including bulky town plans, OS maps (unless they are referred to) and specimens as they will be expensive to post (Figure 40.4).

A bibliography is a list of any written sources of information you have used. Give the name, author, publisher and the date of publication

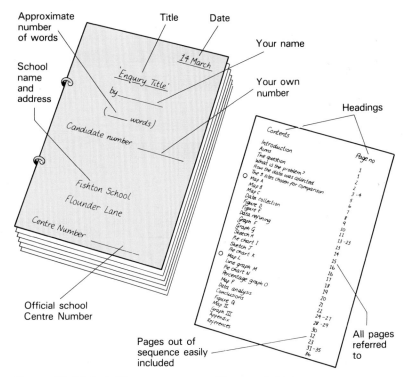

Figure 40.3(a) *A title-page*   **Figure 40.3(b)** *A contents page*

Figure 40.4 *Large, bulky packages are expensive to post – and not popular with postmen!*

41 The final checklist

Enquiries can be divided into three sections.
1 preparation
2 fieldwork
3 follow-up (Figure 41.1).

Figure 41.1
A route to a successful enquiry

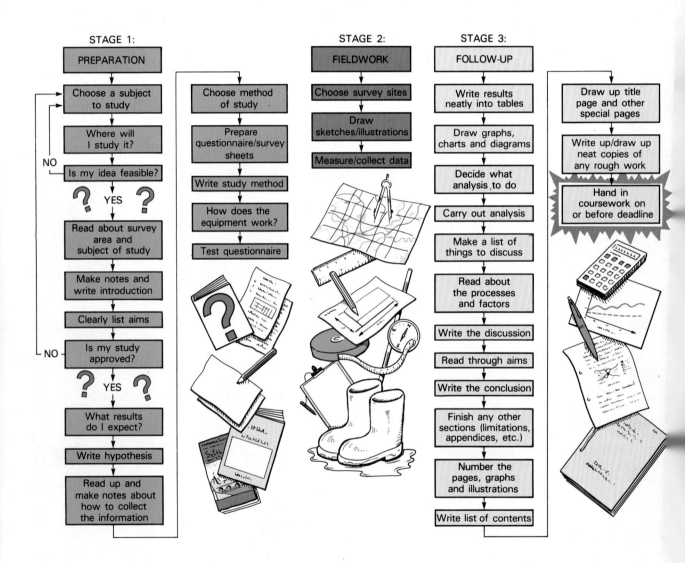

STAGE 1:

PREPARATION

- Choose a subject to study
- Where will I study it?
- Is my idea feasible?
- NO
- **?** YES **?**
- Read about survey area and subject of study
- Make notes and write introduction
- Clearly list aims
- NO
- Is my study approved?
- **?** YES **?**
- What results do I expect?
- Write hypothesis
- Read up and make notes about how to collect the information

- Choose method of study
- Prepare questionnaire/survey sheets
- Write study method
- How does the equipment work?
- Test questionnaire

STAGE 2:

FIELDWORK

- Choose survey sites
- Draw sketches/illustrations
- Measure/collect data

STAGE 3:

FOLLOW-UP

- Write results neatly into tables
- Draw graphs, charts and diagrams
- Decide what analysis to do
- Carry out analysis
- Make a list of things to discuss
- Read about the processes and factors
- Write the discussion
- Read through aims
- Write the conclusion
- Finish any other sections (limitations, appendices, etc.)
- Number the pages, graphs and illustrations
- Write list of contents

- Draw up title page and other special pages
- Write up/draw up neat copies of any rough work
- Hand in coursework on or before deadline

ME FINAL
UGGESTIONS

ep a list of:
- sources of information
- books you have used
- people who have helped you.

e completed coursework should be
tened together with tags or else
ced in a light folder (Figure 41.2).

Make sure your name and candidate
number are marked clearly on the
cover of your coursework.

Quality not **quantity** is important.
Some syllabuses specify a maximum
number of words. You don't need to
count the number of words; an
estimate will do.

Figure 41.2 *The completed coursework*

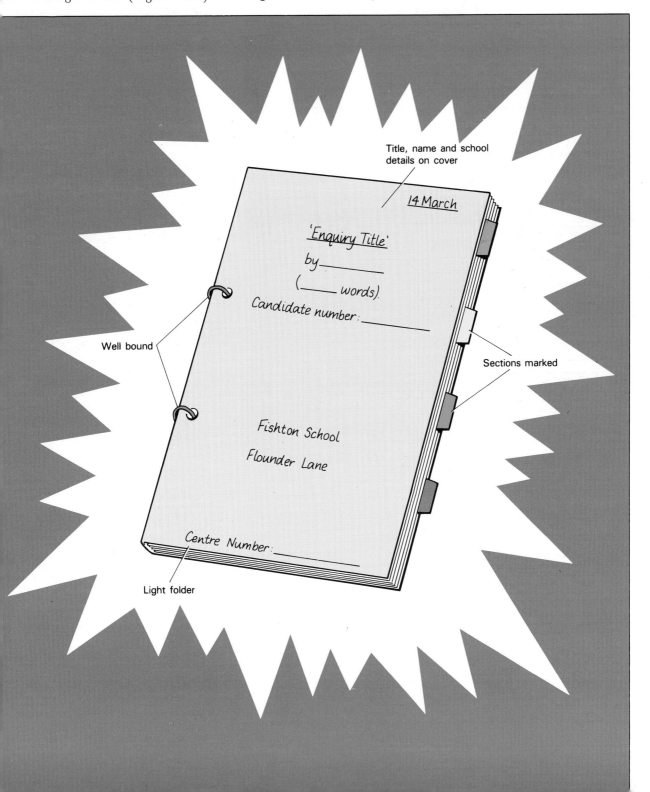

42 Structured exercises

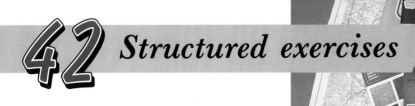

Figure 42.1 *Types of geographical data*

WIND PARKS CAUSE A STORM

The Central Electricity Generating Board today announced proposals for major investment in the development of wind energy. The Board has designated 5 onshore sites and 10 offshore sites for the setting up of Wind Parks.

Wind Parks are groups of about 25 wind machines. The first parks will be 3–4 sq km in area and produce up to 8 megawatts of electricity. It is suggested that wind energy could produce up to 5% of Britain's energy in future, thus saving on fossil fuels.

The wind turbines would be 30 metres high and be placed in exposed and therefore visible locations. The Countryside Commission says that the landscape will be seriously affected, and that many of the proposed sites are in Areas of Outstanding Natural Beauty.

The visual impact of the Wind Parks will pose many problems. Future developments could mean machines as high as 100 metres and it would be impossible to hide these by planting trees. Noise and radio/TV interference would also be major factors to con-sider. One solution is to choose very remote sites, but these would create problems of access.

Figure 42.2

Things to do

Read the article in Figure 42.2.
1 List the main points the article makes.

2 Who does the problem concern?

3 Now write a summary of the information provided.

4 Why might remote sites be most valuable?

5 Comment on the reliability of the information.

Some syllabuses have coursework in which you have to write about information you are given. This can be either analysing data or a decision-making exercise (DME).

ANALYSING DATA

Figure 42.1 shows some of the types of geographical data you could be given to analyse. Information will usually be either audio-visual (sometimes with photographs), a video and slides, or written or drawn material.

It is important that you understand the information you are dealing with and where it comes from. You should then:

● list the main points
● read through and underline what you have been asked to do
● identify from what point of view you are supposed to write your answer.

DECISION-MAKING EXERCISES (DME)

A decision-making exercise normally has five parts:
1 Describe a problem or series of problems. (Do this by selecting information to justify any comments that you make.)
2 Pick out main facts and trends to back up your suggestions.
3 Suggest some alternatives to solve the problems raised.
4 Predict the possible effects of your preferred solution.
5 Comment on the opinions and attitudes of all the people involved in the issue.

Decision-making exercises involve writing a report. Key points to check are:
● how much time is allowed
● what is the word limit
● what conditions you will be working in
● whether preparation time is allowed
● what reference books, atlases, etc. can be used.

SETTING OUT THE PROBLEM

Some questions you may need to answer are:
● What is the problem you have been set?
● When did it occur?
● How often does it occur?
● Who is affected?
● Can the problem be predicted?
● How reliable is the information?
● What factors are important?
● What needs to be done?
● How urgent is it?

WHAT ARE THE ALTERNATIVES?

List all the possible solutions to the problem that you can think of. This will include large scale, major improvements as well as those which are likely to have only small effects.

Discuss each proposal you have made. What are the likely costs and benefits it will bring? Comment on who will be affected and what the likely effects might be.

You may be asked to suggest where your improvements should be made. You can do this by drawing a map showing the areas of greatest need, and by discussing where side effects might result and how the bad ones could be avoided.

MAKING YOUR CHOICE

Some places and schemes will not be suitable. Propose the scheme that you think would be best.
● State your decision.
● List the advantages that it will bring.
Describe the effects you think your decision will have (a diagram or map may be useful, see Figure 42.4).

Things to do

Study Figure 42.3.

1 What does it suggest about the size of the problem and its frequency?

2 Make a list of physical and human factors which could be important in determining the amount of damage earthquakes cause.

3 Units 43, 44 and 45 give three examples of decision-making exercises for you to do.

Figure 42.3 *Earthquakes: problem, size and frequency*

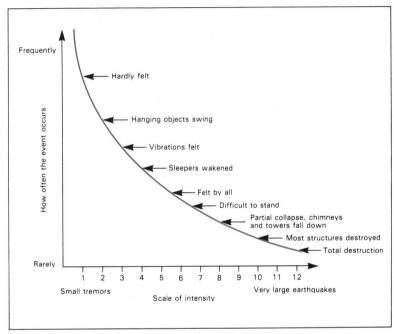

Figure 42.4 *Locating the best solution*

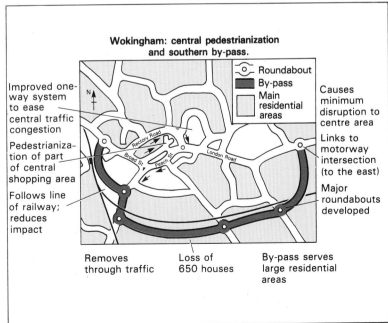

43 *A planning problem: city development*

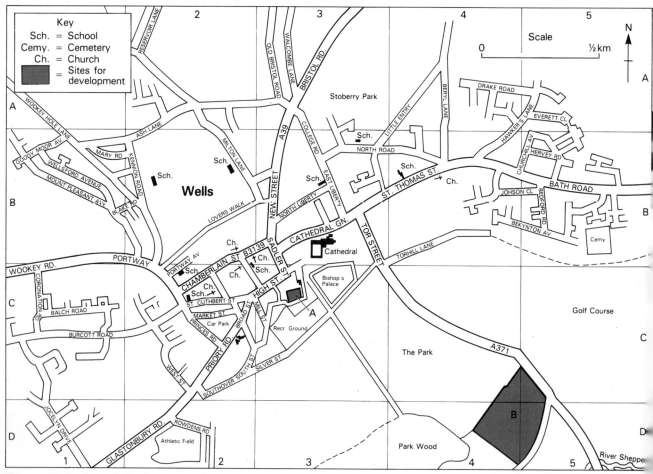

Figure 43.1 *Map of the location of Wells*

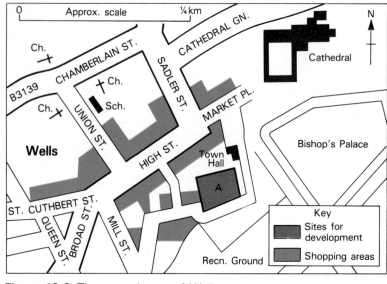

Figure 43.2 *The central area of Wells*

INTRODUCTION

Wells is a city 21 miles south of Bristol by road (Figure 43.1). It has a beautiful 12th century cathedral and a number of important protected buildings. Wells has developed as an important market town for the surrounding population, but shopping facilities are still said to be in need of improvement. Wells is also an important tourist centre, attracting many visitors, especially during the summer.

A busy main road passes through the central shopping street (Figure 43.2). There is only limited space for parking and deliveries in and near the centre. Traffic delays are common.

Increased demands have been made for better leisure and recreational facilities in the city, but little land has been available to do this.

As the city grows in population, demands for more houses will increase. The area has an ageing population (Figure 43.3) which will need more special facilities in the future, including hospitals and nursing homes.

A site near the city centre has become available for redevelopment (site A, Figures 43.1 and 43.2). You are part of a planning team who have been asked to make a detailed proposal to the local council for the development of this site.

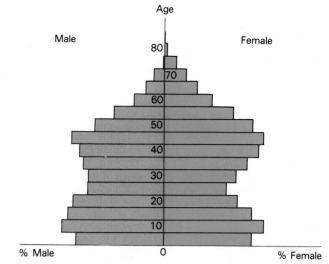

Figure 43.3 Population pyramid for Wells

Structured exercise

1 a Describe the planning problem with which you are faced.
   b Some possible alternative strategies are shown in the headlines in Figure 43.4. For each proposal, suggest which people would most benefit from the changes and who would be most likely to object to them.
   c What restrictions do you think will need to be placed on building height and design?
   d In your view, which of the alternatives would be best? Justify your decision.
   e How do you think the interested groups shown in Figure 43.5 would react to your decision?
   f What problems might your decision bring to the centre of Wells?
   g What other information would have been useful to help you make your decision?

2 If a second, much larger site became available further from the city centre (site B in Figure 43.1, square 5C), suggest what it might be used for and what services would be needed.

Meeting to discuss leisure strategy

Surgery scheme

Scheme for flats

Shoppers deserting the city!

Outcry at leisure survey proposals

Parking blitz

New market

Report is awaited on sports centre siting

NO PARKING – NO TRADE

Wells is losing business and can no longer cope with special events because of ridiculously inadequate parking facilities.

This is the view of local shoppers and traders who say it is small wonder the city is losing the battle against out-of-town shops with adjacent car parks.

Figure 43.4 Alternative strategies

Local residents   Local business people   Conservationists

Figure 43.5 Interested groups

44 *Flood control: protecting the coastline*

OVER 280 DIE IN EAST COAST FLOODS

More than 280 people lost their lives and many hundreds are missing through floods which ravaged the East Coast of Britain early yesterday. Thousands were made homeless when the sea, whipped by a hurricane, smashed coast defences, and a wall of water, in some cases 8ft high, poured inland.

Figure 44.1 *Newspaper article from* The Daily Telegraph, *2 February 1953*

Flooding is a great hazard along the east coast of England (Figure 44.1). High winds led to a tidal surge on the night of 31 January 1953. As a result, 307 people were drowned and an area of 850 square kilometres was flooded.

Human activities as well as natural forces have made the east coast a high risk area for flooding. Many landscape changes have altered local conditions and increased the chances of flooding (Figure 44.2).

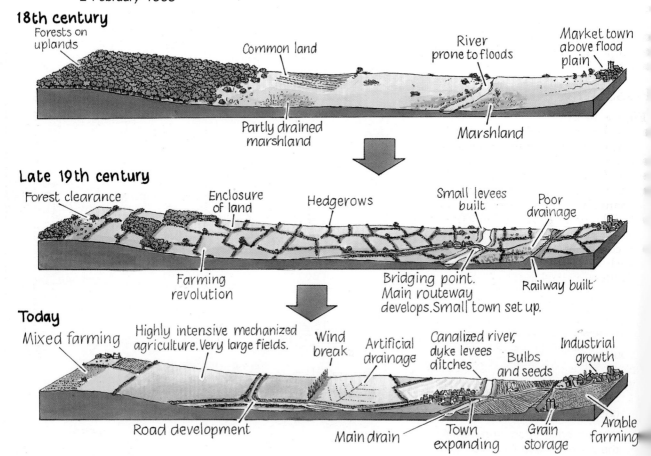

Increasing water use for settlements. Soil shrinks and cracks as it dries.

Figure 44.2 *Landscape changes in East Anglia*

Things to do

1 Describe the landscape changes shown in Figure 44.2.

2 Look at the causes of flooding listed and then explain how each of the changes affects the water cycle in Figure 29.3 on page 61.

CAUSES

- downwarping (sinking) of the North Sea basin
- tidal changes, dredging, dumping and reclamation
- high spring tides
- strong onshore winds causing tidal surges
- heavy rainstorms, snowmelt, frozen ground
- low lying land, poor coastal defences
- straightened rivers, drains and urban areas
- changes in vegetation, fewer trees.

EFFECTS

- faster river flows, greater energy in rivers, more erosion and deposition
- communications cut
- crop damage
- salt contamination of soil and ground water
- paralysis of waterside industry
- property damage and loss
- loss of life.

POSSIBLE SOLUTIONS

Figure 44.4)
- restrict the use of land by local planning and building regulations
- construct walls on the coast
- build levees or dykes around rivers
- have overflows or diversion channels for floodwater to escape
- build storage dams to hold river water
- a complete coastal defence plan, such as the Delta Plan for the Polders in Holland.

Structured exercise

You have been asked to draw up a plan to reduce the risk of flooding in the area shown in Figure 44.4.

1 Draw a map to show the areas of greatest flood risk.

2 Write a brief report to describe the conditions which would cause flooding and identify which people would be worst hit.

3 Discuss the possible ways of protecting:
   a coastal areas
   b farmland .
   c urban areas.

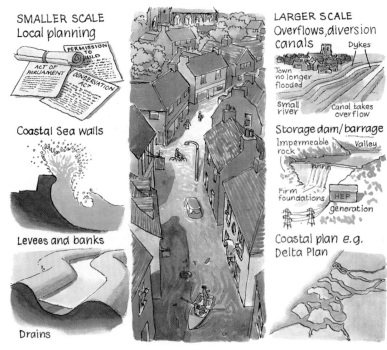

Figure 44.3 Flooding: some possible solutions

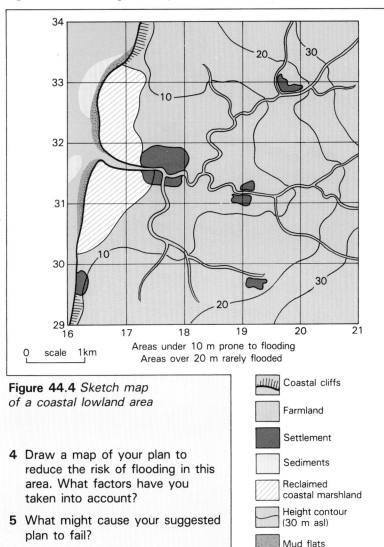

Figure 44.4 Sketch map of a coastal lowland area

Areas under 10 m prone to flooding
Areas over 20 m rarely flooded

4 Draw a map of your plan to reduce the risk of flooding in this area. What factors have you taken into account?

5 What might cause your suggested plan to fail?

45 Supplying water

Elapakkam in Southern India is an area of drought and flood, largely because of the monsoon (Figure 45.1). Monsoon areas have a wet and a dry season. Winds from the ocean bring heavy rains, while very dry weather dominates from the north.

Elapakkam has been ravaged by a cyclone and flood. Improvements and rebuilding are needed (Figures 45.2 and 45.3). Money has been raised and local help and advice has been given by workers from a non-governmental organization (NGO).

Figure 45.1
The Asian monsoon

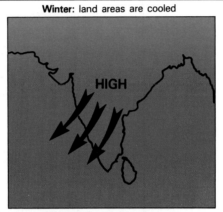

Winter: land areas are cooled

HIGH

High pressure forms over India.
Winds blow off the land.
The **dry** monsoon.

Summer: land areas are hot

LOW

Low pressure forms over the land.
Winds are sucked in from the ocean.
The **wet** monsoon.

Figure 45.2 *Part of a letter from a local priest*

The climax of the calamity was on the 12th November. I do not know what to write or how to explain what has happened. Seventy to eighty year old people say they have not seen such a calamity in their lifetime.

The storm started on the early morning of the 3rd, with heavy rains continuing without a break for 9 days. On the 12th there was the cyclone, killing hundreds of people, thousands of cattle, sheep, cows and bulls. It destroyed thousands of huts and uprooted trees. It completely cut our area off from the rest of the country, destroying bridges, railway lines, electricity and washing away all villages.

Figure 45.3
Headline from the Indian Express

FLOODS DROWN 600 VILLAGES

Reservoirs were empty after the drought. With heavy rain, they then filled to the brim and their walls were topped, sending a wave of flood water over the already saturated ground. Most surface drinking water was contaminated and in the days that followed, the uncontaminated water quickly ran dry.

Key

HWM Mean high-water mark

LWM Mean low-water mark

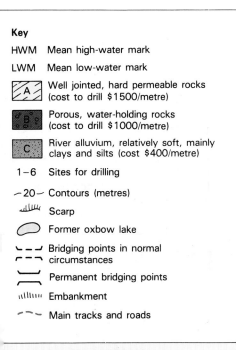

A Well jointed, hard permeable rocks (cost to drill $1500/metre)

B Porous, water-holding rocks (cost to drill $1000/metre)

C River alluvium, relatively soft, mainly clays and silts (cost $400/metre)

1–6 Sites for drilling

—20— Contours (metres)

ᴧᴧᴧ Scarp

⬭ Former oxbow lake

- - - Bridging points in normal circumstances

╪ Permanent bridging points

ᴧ|ᴧ|ᴧ Embankment

- ~ - Main tracks and roads

STRUCTURED EXERCISE

The village must have a reliable supply of water. You are the head of an engineering team who have been contracted to site and build a well.

Study the geological profile and contour map of the area (Figure 45.4) and answer these questions.

1 Under what conditions will there be a permanent supply of water?

2 Where will you have to drill down to, to get permanent water?

3 Measure the well depth and distance from the village for each drilling site. Calculate the construction costs for each well and complete the table (Figure 45.5) for the six possible sites.

4 Write a report to outline the advantages and disadvantages of each well site.

5 How and why might the views of local people and government officials differ from yours?

6 What problems might result from your chosen well site?

Figure 45.5 *Where to drill: factors to consider*

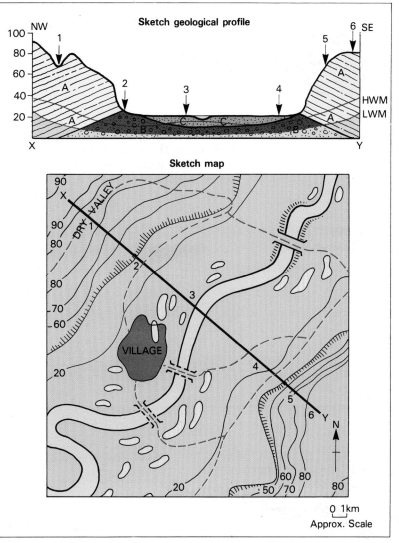

Figure 45.4 *Geological profile and relief map of the area*

Well site	Location	Other factors to consider	Well depth	Construction Costs (C)	Distance to well	Distance costs (D) $1000/km	Total cost ($) (D & C)
1	Dry valley Hard permeable rocks Road access OK	Costs $1500/m Far from village Secure well					
2	River terrace Porous rocks Underneath geology uncertain	Costs $1000/m Easy access Above normal flood limit					
3	Close to river On alluvium, soft rocks Prone to flooding	Easiest location Surface costs $400/m Close to village					
4	Edge of flood plain On alluvium Occasional flooding	Reasonable access under normal conditions Surface costs $400/m					
5	On scarp slope Permeable	Costs $1500/m Access very difficult Water supply excellent					
6	On scarp top Permeable Hard Rocks	Costs $1500/m Access difficult Water supply excellent					

46 Timed essays

Figure 46.1
Taking the title apart

Who? Where? Why? Compare
Contrast Describe
Examine   Account for
What?   Identify
Diagrams   Explain Discuss
Annotate   Examples
Outline   Illustrate

Figure 46.2
An essay plan

The key words.   What must I write about?

What must be done?

Describe the main processes which cause glaciated features in mountain regions → Where? } Title

1. Freeze/thaw   } paragraph
2. Corrosion 3. Plucking } headings
4. Pressure   5. Melting

} What headings must I write under?

Key words in the centre of the page

THE MAIN PROCESSES = What was happening?

Where?

Describe: = WHAT are they?   mountains

Plan linked up by arrows

What is the question about?

Examples
Lake District
Scottish Uplands
North Wales
New Zealand

Use a variety of places

Coursework can include essays done under examination conditions with a time limit. You will usually be able to prepare the subject, but not know the exact title.

WHAT THE QUESTION SAYS

Take the title apart. Do this by underlining the words in the title which tell you exactly what you are supposed to do. These are the **key words** (Figure 46.1).

PREPARATION AND PLANNING

Organize your ideas before you begin writing your essay. Spend a few moments writing a list of things you want to say. Then put them in order by either numbering the points or linking them up with arrows (Figure 46.2). If you leave enough space, you can always add to your plan as you write your essay.

Your essay plan should:
● be spread out on a page
● contain short phrases not sentences
● be based on the **key words** in the title.

ESSAY TECHNIQUE

- Start by defining what you will be writing about. Do not spend very long on this – one or two short paragraphs will do.
- Essays should be based on *your* ideas. They must also have facts you have learnt and examples to illustrate the points you make.
- Use well-labelled diagrams and maps to make your answer clear.
- Start each point with a new paragraph.
- Unless you are asked to, don't spend too long on one point.
- Try to balance your discussion. Use a variety of case studies from different parts of the world.
- Make sure you answer the question directly.
- If you have two equal parts to answer, spend half the time on each.
- When one part of the question has more marks, you should spend more time on it. The greater the number of marks available, the longer you need to spend.

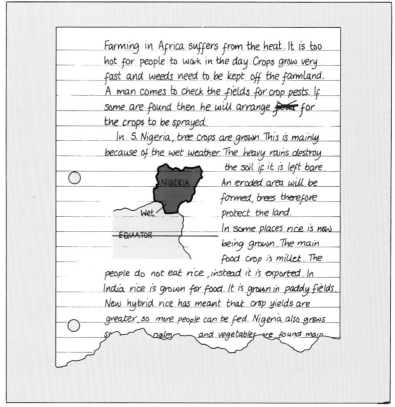

Figure 46.3 *Part of an essay*

Things to do

1 Figure 46.3 shows part of an essay. Write a list of good and bad points about it.

2 Write out all the essay questions (Figure 46.4) and underline their key words.

3 Study the checklist (Figure 46.5). For any two of the essays in Figure 46.4:
   a write an essay plan
   b make a list of the examples you would use to illustrate your ideas.

4 Write a 45 minute essay from one of your two plans.

---

1 (a) What is population migration? (5)
  (b) Use examples to explain what causes people to migrate. (15)

2 Use examples to describe what industries are found at ports and why they are there. (20)

3 (a) What is subsistence farming? (5)
  (b) Use a detailed example to illustrate the problems these farmers have. (15)

4 What factors affect the temperature of the earth's surface? (20)

5 (a) How do landslides occur? (10)
  (b) What can be done to try to control them? (10)

6 What causes coastlines to be eroded into different shapes? (20)

7 (a) Why do cities have great transport problems? (12)
  (b) Outline how ONE city you have studied has tried to cope with its transport problems. (8)

Figure 46.4 *Some essay questions (marks are shown in brackets)*

---

1 What subject area am I being tested on? _____ ☐

2 When is the essay? _____ ☐

3 Will I get time to prepare? _____ ☐

4 Will I be given the title before? ___ ☐

5 What sources of information can I use? _____ ☐

6 How much time will I get to write it? _____ ☐

7 Will I get time to plan the essay? _____ ☐

8 Can I use references or is it to be done under exam conditions? ____ ☐

9 Will I get a choice? _____ ☐

10 Will graphics, photographs or diagrams be given to me? _____ ☐

Figure 46.5 *Checklist: writing essays*

Index